ABID HASAN SAFRANI

ABID HASAN SAFRANI
Netaji's Comrade-in-Arms

Compiled by
Ismat Mehdi and Shehbaz Safrani

Foreword by
Sugata Bose

Orient BlackSwan

ABID HASAN SAFRANI: NETAJI'S COMRADE-IN-ARMS

ORIENT BLACKSWAN PRIVATE LIMITED

Registered Office
3-6-752 Himayatnagar, Hyderabad 500 029, Telangana, India
e-mail: centraloffice@orientblackswan.com

Other Offices
Bengaluru, Chennai, Guwahati, Hyderabad, Kolkata,
Mumbai, New Delhi, Noida, Patna, Visakhapatnam

First published by Orient Blackswan Private Limited 2023

ISBN 978-93-5442-605-6

037228

Typeset in
Adobe Garamond Pro 11.5/13
by Le Studio Graphique, Gurgaon 122 001

Printed in India at
Thomson Press, New Delhi 110 020

Published by
Orient Blackswan Private Limited
3-6-752 Himayatnagar, Hyderabad 500 029, Telangana, India
e-mail: info@orientblackswan.com

Dedicated to the memory of
Begum Amir Hasan (Ammajan)
A strong believer in the value of freedom,
education and selfless service

CONTENTS

PHOTOGRAPHS

FOREWORD

A Quiet Revolutionary

SUGATA BOSE

It was January 1970. You can imagine the thrill of a boy just entering his teens on being told that Netaji Subhas Chandra Bose's sole Indian companion on his perilous 90-day submarine voyage from Europe to Asia in 1943 was coming to stay with his family. We happily vacated the children's room as we were duty-bound to do whenever Netaji's close associates visited Calcutta. This room, on the ground floor at 1 Woodburn Park, was better known as 'Nehru's Room' because that was where Jawaharlal stayed as Sarat Chandra Bose's guest during his visits to Calcutta during the freedom struggle. We were familiar with Abid Hasan's photographs with his leader on the deck of the German submarine and their transfer together mid-ocean on a rubber boat to the Japanese submarine. They were prominently displayed at the museum in Netaji Bhawan. His hair had greyed, but it was easy to recognise Netaji's comrade-in-arms when he arrived at our home, with a smile on his lips and a twinkle in his eyes, and endeared himself to us in an instant.

My father, Sisir Kumar Bose, Netaji's charioteer in his *mahanishkraman* or great escape from Calcutta in January 1941, had invited Abid Hasan on behalf of the Netaji Research Bureau (NRB) to deliver the Netaji Oration on 23 January 1970. He had started this Netaji birth anniversary tradition in January 1961 when S. A. Ayer, the minister of publicity in the Azad Hind Government, had delivered the first Netaji Oration. These January orations were initially designed to record for posterity firsthand memoirs of those who had fought alongside Netaji for India's freedom. In this tradition, S. A. Ayer had been followed among

Netaji's close associates by M. R. Vyas in 1962, Hari Vishnu Kamath in 1963, Lakshmi Sahgal in 1964, Girija K. Mookerjee in 1965, Prem Kumar Sahgal in 1966, and Alexander Werth in 1969. This is not to mention the visits of Jawaharlal Nehru, Jaya Prakash Narain, and Dilip Kumar Roy over the years and Khan Abdul Ghaffar Khan, who had visited as recently as December 1969. As soon as Abid Hasan retired from the Indian Foreign Service after his final assignment as Ambassador to Denmark, Sisir Kumar Bose made certain that he be brought to Calcutta in January 1970.

Uncle Abid's room had a door leading to the beautiful curved southern verandah of 1 Woodburn Park. That is where we gathered around him, as he sat on a cane chair looking at the eucalyptus tree in the distance, to hear him narrate his adventures with Netaji in Europe, the Atlantic and Indian Oceans, and Asia. The devotion and loyalty that Netaji elicited from his followers had to be seen to be believed. As with most other men and women of the Indian National Army (INA) that I have met, Uncle Abid wept profusely as he remembered his leader. He had not yet written his oration when he arrived in Calcutta. He was provided with a desk and chair, along with my mother Krishna Bose's Olivetti typewriter, in one corner of the verandah. My mother was pleased to find someone who could beat her in the art of slow typing. After composing a passage, Uncle Abid would give us a shout and we would rush to hear what he had written. After reading a few sentences, his voice would choke with emotion. He became concerned that he would not be able to deliver the oration before the public. 'How embarrassing it would be if I break down like this,' he kept saying. My mother tried to boost his morale with a steady supply of good food and music. He enjoyed Bengali cuisine supplemented by a bowl of green chilies placed before him. I watched him sitting at the oval marble table in our dining room, with beads of sweat appearing on his forehead as he munched the chilies and tears flowed down his cheeks.

After a hard day's work Uncle Abid would say to my mother in the evening, 'Krishna-ji, now please sing.' My mother had an exquisite singing voice. Uncle Abid wanted to hear two favourites.

The first was Rabindranath Tagore's '*Tomay sajabo jatane kusum ratane keure kankane kumkume chandane*' (I will adorn you lovingly with flowers and jewels, perfumes and bangles, vermillion and sandal paste). The other was a song composed by Mohini Chowdhuri and set to music by Shailesh Dattagupta: '*Tomay ami bhulbo na go, tomar katha roibe mone, naiba holo milan moder ei jibane*' (I will not forget you, you will be remembered, no matter our union eluded us in this life). Having sung the same two songs seven days in a row, Mamma asked Uncle Abid whether they held any special significance for him. He just liked the first song, in which Tagore had beautifully expressed man's eternal love for woman. But yes, there was a particular reason behind his fondness for the second song, he said, looking wistful as he hummed its first line. Observing the serious expression on his face, my mother could not bring herself to ask who he would not forget—a lost love or his lost leader. Having heard the refrain 'I will not forget' from so many of Netaji's followers, she concluded that the balance of probability lay with the latter.[1] After reading this book, I am not so sure. Despite his deep devotion to his leader, the song may have evoked memories of the woman Uncle Abid had courted in wartime Berlin and who might have occasionally come to visit him in post-war Switzerland.

On the morning of 23 January 1970, at Netaji Bhawan, Abid Hasan delivered his beautifully crafted and deeply moving Netaji Oration titled 'The Men from Imphal' in a somewhat monotonous voice, struggling not to be overcome by emotion. He had chosen to foreground in his oration the harrowing retreat of the brave soldiers of freedom after their march towards Delhi had been halted at Imphal. In one brilliant paragraph he portrayed the character of the army of liberation to which he belonged:

> What a group we were and ours was but a unit among many of its kind in our army. I felt proud and I feel more proud today that I belonged to it. Baluchis were there among us, and Assamese, Kashmiris and Malayalis, Pathans and Sikhs and Gujeratis, proud members of classes called the martial and those till then denied reputation for martial valour but who proved in battle that they could by their deeds claim

> equal honour. Every region in India was represented and every religion and every caste, mixed inseparably together not only in bigger formations but even in small platoons and sections, each unit being a living tribute to the unity of India. We had our different private faiths and we had our different languages, but in our purpose and in our political belief we were a well-knit, determined and indivisible whole.[2]

And once they reached Mandalay, Netaji came to meet them: 'The Sikhs oiled their beards, the Punjabi Muslims, the Dogras and Rajputs twirled their moustaches and we the indiscriminate put on as good a face as we could manage.' As Netaji spoke to them their weariness seemed to depart and they 'felt refreshing new blood circulating' in their veins. Abid Hasan understood the essence of his leadership: 'He was all we had, our leader to whom each one of us however humble meant something and who to us all meant everything. He belonged to us, to us all of the Azad Hind Movement and entirely without any compromise.'[3]

Abid Hasan then flashed back to October 1943 to illustrate the meaning of 'without any compromise' by telling the story of Netaji's visit to the Chettiar temple in Singapore. He had turned away the head priest, saying: 'What! Come to your temple where even Hindus of other castes are not permitted entry, not to speak of members of other communities who are equally near and dear to me?' He agreed to go when the high priest returned with an invitation to 'an Indian national demonstration'. 'When we came to the temple,' Abid Hasan remembered, 'I found it filled to capacity with the uniforms of the INA officers and men and the black caps of South Indian Muslims glaringly evident.' In his 1970 Oration, he said that he did not remember the speech that Netaji gave on that occasion: 'The memory I retain is one of an invigorating music as that of a symphony dedicated to the unity of the motherland.'[4] That music sustained him during his travails on the battlefield. It appears that he did keep a record of that historic speech by Netaji that the editors have found in his papers and included in this volume.

Not all of the anecdotes he narrated to us in the southern verandah of 1 Woodburn Park, especially details of the submarine voyage and daily life with Netaji in Singapore and Rangoon, could find place in Abid Hasan's Netaji Oration. We urged him to write his memoirs; otherwise precious vignettes of our history would be lost to future generations. 'Krishna-ji, why are you so impatient?' he asked my mother.[5] He was now going to lead a retired life and set up a farm and orchard in southern India. We were going to visit his farm and he would record his life's experiences at leisure. By the time he returned to Calcutta a few years later, our Woodburn Park home had been acquired by the government. My father had hastily bought a two-storied house at 90 Sarat Bose Road, which was in a rather dilapidated condition. My mother named it 'Basundhara' and set about restoring it and making it a centre of academic, cultural and political activity as Woodburn Park had been.

On 10 March 1976, Abid Hasan came to dinner at 'Basundhara'. Placing a basketful of grapes from Hyderabad in front of my mother, he stood with bowed head. He confessed that his history had not been written; he had failed to keep his word. He knew he deserved punishment for his failure and so had brought this *nazrana*.[6] My mother's diary records 'a very nice garden party' on the evening of 12 March, at which Abid Hasan and M. R. Vyas were present along with some twenty-five guests. 'A colourful Darbari Shamiana was put up,' Krishna writes. 'My Tagar tree and Rakta Karabi were in bloom.'[7] On the morning of 13 March Abid Hasan shifted from his hotel and came to stay with us.[8] We were determined to record his memoirs on this occasion. We were ready with pen and paper and, more importantly, my father's tape recorder. My mother hung a photograph of Netaji addressing the Greater East Asia Conference in November 1943 on the wall of his guest suite. We had seen Abid Hasan in the film footage of the conference, arranging Netaji's papers. Surely the picture would inspire him to recount his experiences of those days. But Uncle Abid said he had starved at the expensive hotel and wanted to be fed first. He ate with great relish the two large *pabda* fish served for him at lunch. He had once said to Netaji, he told us, that it was impossible to identify him as a Bengali, except when he ate fish.[9]

The extended interview with Abid Hasan, that formed the basis of Krishna Bose's long-form article 'Sainiker Smriti' and later published as 'A Soldier Remembers' in the NRB's journal *The Oracle*, was conducted day and night between 13 and 15 March 1976. Uncle Abid was a diffident public speaker but a very engaging conversationalist. Puffing an endless chain of cigarettes and sipping cold beer, he transported us over those days and nights to the military camps of the Indian Legion in Germany, the rehearsal of the national greeting 'Jai Hind' with Netaji, the drama and discipline of the submarine voyage, the tumultuous public events and the intimate private moments with Netaji during the Azad Hind movement in Southeast Asia, and the saga in Imphal. During the submarine voyage Netaji dictated a speech to Abid Hasan that he would deliver to the women of the Rani of Jhansi Regiment of his dreams. Once during a quiet moment up on the bridge of the German submarine, Abid Hasan had asked Netaji to name the worst fate he might suffer. Netaji had answered promptly, 'To be in exile'. This, as he prepared to mobilise Indian expatriates and proclaim a government in exile in Southeast Asia for a great patriotic war. Upon their transfer from the German to the Japanese submarine, both Netaji and Abid Hasan had felt 'something akin to a home-coming'.[10]

In the evening Uncle Abid wanted a break and announced his intention to go shopping for Bengal's *Tangail* saris with my mother. By the time she got ready, he had changed his mind and wanted to buy a Golden Retriever puppy instead, having seen an advertisement in *The Statesman* newspaper. The puppies were located but their owner was drunk, making it impossible to negotiate a purchase. My mother then called friends who were members of the Calcutta Kennel Club for help. They were later able to find a lovely Golden Retriever puppy named Andy for Uncle Abid.[11] My mother's diary contains an important entry on 14 March regarding the tape-recording session throughout that day. 'Abid Hasan says,' she notes,

> on 17th August 1945 in Saigon he would have accompanied Netaji—and Netaji himself wished so but because of military protocol Col. Habibur Rahman was asked to go. He was senior. Anyway—all of them were to follow him shortly—so they did not realise that it would become a matter of such importance at the moment.[12]

On 15 March morning, Pandit Ravi Shankar came to see the Netaji Museum and we went to Netaji Bhawan to show him round. As with most visitors, he was deeply moved to see the documentary film footage of Netaji. On 23 January he had presented a wonderful Netaji Birthday Concert for NRB, performing the ragas *Shyamkalyan*, *Charukeshi* and *Majhkhambaj* on the occasion of the Second International Netaji Seminar (the first had been held in 1973) that had featured Dilip Kumar Roy, Teruo Hachiya, Prem Kumar Sahgal and Gurbaksh Singh Dhillon. My parents and I had resumed our tape-recording session with Uncle Abid at home in the afternoon when news came that my B.A. Part 1 results were out. After the marathon interview was over, it was time to indulge Uncle Abid. 'Hasan Saab and myself went to Bangasree,' my mother has recorded, 'and bought four saris'. They then went and visited my mother's parents.[13]

'At about 4.30 am in the morning,' says the entry for 16 March 1976 of my mother's reliable diary, 'Abid Hasan left for Hyderabad'. He remonstrated with my mother as she appeared at that unearthly hour with a cup of tea, followed by us. 'You too?' he said looking at us. 'Well, I am your driver,' I told him. 'How else will you get to the airport?' Uncle Abid, my father, my sister and I got into our black Studebaker Champion and set off for the airport. Mamma remained at home with my brother. She waved from the balcony upstairs and heard 'Jai Hind, Jai Hind' in the darkness as Uncle Abid said his good-byes to the staff. 'It was good to have Abid Hasan with us for a few days,' she noted. 'It was a welcome distraction from our material worries.'[14]

I left for Cambridge in September 1978 and was not always present during Uncle Abid's subsequent visits to Calcutta. It was during one of these visits that my mother and he settled on the conclusion to 'Sainiker Smriti'. Uncle Abid interrupted a discourse on flowers to tell my mother that he had suffered his usual fate with Netaji at their final meeting in Saigon airport on 17 August 1945: he had received a scolding for arriving late with the luggage. My mother responded with the Bengali saying: '*Shasan kora tarei saje sohag kore je go*' (It is only the one who showers affection who is entitled to issue a rebuke). Uncle Abid laughed and replied: 'I don't know about that. That is your interpretation.'[15]

Uncle Abid remained a pillar of support for my father as he struggled against tremendous odds to preserve and disseminate the finest lessons of our freedom movement. On receiving the NRB's new journal *The Oracle*, Abid Hasan wrote from Golkonda, Hyderabad, on 8 December 1979:

> My dear Sisir,
>
> Thanks ever so much for sending me a copy of The Oracle. You have brought it out very well indeed—much better than I expected. But then you are always so thorough and painstaking attending to all minute details, just like your uncle and it is this drudgery of attending to details that pays dividends in the end. I know so many people envy you when success is achieved but of course they are not there to help you with a hand at the wheel pulling the cart out when it is stuck in the mire. How many years, day in and day out have you been attending to the Netaji Seminar? It is thanks mainly to your efforts that it has now turned out to be a veritable scholarly research institute.
>
> My heartiest congratulations to you.
>
> With kindest regards,
>
> Yours,
>
> Abid Hasan[16]

In 1983, INA veterans including Abid Hasan and my father fell victim to a classic act of British perfidy. My father had been always prepared to help genuine scholars and filmmakers on Netaji, beginning with Hugh Toye in the 1950s and Hemen Gupta in the 1960s, and he respected their academic and artistic freedom. The film by Granada TV in 1983 was, however, a deliberate and egregious case of deception, deviating wildly from the script. The director used tiny snippets of lengthy interviews with Netaji's associates in an attempt to gain legitimacy while giving much more airtime to trenchant and uninformed critics of Netaji and the INA. Abid Hasan wrote to Sisir on 13 January 1984:

> All the sincere work you, Krishna and your band of devoted followers of Netaji have done during the past so many years brought you some recognition and in much greater proportion, the envy of others. That these people should now seize opportunity to malign you has to be accepted ... Now we can do nothing more than publicly dissociate ourselves from the film—our intention was sincere and we shall ride out the storm.[17]

'I shall of course stand by you,' Abid Hasan assured Sisir Kumar Bose, closing with the immortal 'Jai Hind'.[18]

My last meeting with Uncle Abid took place in 1983. I was by that time a Fellow of St. Catharine's College at the University of Cambridge. After several poverty-stricken years as a student, I had something of an income and decided to treat my father and Uncle Abid to a sumptuous dinner at Salloo's in Knightsbridge, London. I think Abid Hasan enjoyed the European wine even more than the South Asian food. Uncle Abid, my father, Ayesha and I talked late into the evening about Gandhi and Jinnah, Independence and Partition, and, of course, the grand vision of subcontinental unity presented by Netaji Subhas Chandra Bose. When I dropped him off at his hotel in our little mustard-coloured Datsun before driving back to Cambridge at midnight, I could not have imagined that he would leave us the following year.

We never forgot him, but India's younger generation needs to be taught about the forgotten vestiges of our freedom struggle. Faced with the threat of unequal citizenship from the forces of religious majoritarianism, my mother wrote her last published article on 1 February 2020,[19] on the values represented by Abid Hasan, before her own passing three weeks later on 22 February 2020. Now C. Narendra Reddy, Ismat Mehdi, Shehbaz Safrani, and Sumanta Banerjee have placed us greatly in their debt by putting together this inspiring volume on Netaji's comrade-in-arms Abid Hasan Safrani. He was a quiet revolutionary who kept himself out of the limelight even while being present at every vital scene and moment of the final phase of our freedom struggle across Europe and Asia. He served his country with distinction after independence in China, West Asia, Africa and Europe.

Fifty years ago, Abid Hasan had in his Netaji Oration referred to 'these frustrating times when India again seems to be a house divided against itself'. The times have turned even more ominous now and the 'inhuman acts' that Abid Hasan had deplored are becoming an everyday reality in today's India. His oration was, in Sisir Kumar Bose's words, 'a moving affirmation of the revolutionary faith given to us by our Leader'. I close this foreword with Abid Hasan's message of hope: 'The people of India will accept any leadership provided the call remains the same, and the call cannot be but—"Forget not that the grossest crime is to compromise with injustice and wrong".'[20]

NOTES

1. Krishna Bose, *Itihaser Sandhane* (Calcutta: Ananda, 1972), 114–115.
2. Abid Hasan Safrani, *The Men from Imphal* (Calcutta: Netaji Research Bureau, 1971), 7.
3. Ibid., 9.
4. Ibid., 10–12.
5. Krishna Bose, 'Sainiker Smriti', in *Prasanga Subhaschandra* (Calcutta: Ananda, 1993), 12.
6. Ibid.; Krishna Bose's Diary, 10 March 1976.
7. Krishna Bose's Diary, 12 March 1976.
8. Krishna Bose's Diary, 13 March 1976.
9. Krishna Bose, 'Sainiker Smriti', in *Prasanga Subhaschandra*, 13.
10. Abid Hasan, 'A Soldier Remembers', *The Oracle* 6(1) (January 1984): 19–20, 22–23. See my description of the submarine voyage in Sugata Bose, *His Majesty's Opponent: Subhas Chandra Bose and India's Struggle against Empire* (Cambridge, MA: The Belknap Press of Harvard University Press, 2011), 231–237.
11. Krishna Bose, 'Sainiker Smriti', in *Prasanga Subhaschandra*, 42–43.
12. Krishna Bose's Diary, 14 March 1976.
13. Krishna Bose's Diary, 23 January 1976, and 15 March 1976.

14. Krishna Bose's Diary, 16 March 1976; Krishna Bose, 'Sainiker Smriti', in *Prasanga Subhaschandra*, 54.

15. Krishna Bose, 'Sainiker Smriti', in *Prasanga Subhaschandra*, 55–56.

16. Abid Hasan to Sisir Kumar Bose, 8 December 1979, reproduced in *The Oracle* 7(1) (January 1985): 61.

17. Abid Hasan to Sisir Kumar Bose, 13 January 1984, reproduced in *The Oracle* 7(1) (January 1985): 61–62.

18. Ibid.

19. Krishna Bose, 'Netajir Sahajoddhara: Abid Hasan, Akbar Shah', *Ananda Bazaar Patrika*, 1 February 2020, in Sumantra Bose (ed.), *Krishna Bose Rachana Sangraha* (Kolkata: Ananda, 2021).

20. Abid Hasan Safrani, *The Men from Imphal*, 'Preface' and p. 18.

PREFACE

Abid Hasan Safrani's life revolved around Netaji Subhas Chandra Bose. He was so close that Netaji chose him to be his sole companion for his historic journey by submarine from Germany to Japan. Safrani came from an old Hyderabad family that was deeply involved in the Indian freedom movement, with his mother playing an important role in the Gandhi-led struggle. He himself highly influenced his family with the thoughts and life of Netaji.

On the occasion of Netaji's 125th birth anniversary, the family decided to pay tribute by writing about Abid Hasan Safrani's life and association with the great leader. It was also felt that Safrani's story needs to be told to fill an important gap in the narration of India's freedom struggle. This becomes more urgent in the current scenario when the reality of India's freedom struggle as a truly secular and democratic movement seems to be fast fading in favour of a diametrically opposed narrative.

The venture to bring out the present book was initiated by C. Narendra Reddy, who is married to Safrani's niece, Kulsum Reddy. Another niece, Professor Ismat Mehdi, and his nephew Shehbaz Safrani joined Narendra. Many other family members contributed in their own way. Professor Mehdi had carefully preserved numerous articles, newspaper cuttings and, most importantly, Safrani's own diaries, scribblings and letters. These turned out to be a great source of information. They helped reconstruct the period and places of old Hyderabad, which fostered a rich socio-cultural life, embracing both Hindus and Muslims and other communities. These fertile environs that shaped the lifestyle and thinking of Abid Hasan Safrani have been described in one of the chapters. This chapter also throws light on another important episode—Hyderabad's association with the famous poet-politician Sarojini Naidu and her father Aghornath Chattopadhyay, both of whom played vital roles in national politics and the freedom struggle.

Another chapter relates the events surrounding Safrani's family during the tumultuous days of the Gandhi-led Swadeshi movement, when members of the family made a bonfire of foreign made goods to demonstrate their patriotic zeal and rejection of British rule. These events impressed upon the mind of the young Safrani as he grew up in Hyderabad in the 1920s. They would later lead him to plunge into active politics when he came under Netaji's influence.

The main body of the book is devoted to Safrani's life with Netaji and his activities under his leadership: the famous submarine journey that took Netaji and him to new shores, the later wartime struggles in Imphal, and the final denouement with the fatal air crash. This narrative sparkles with Safrani's own words that bring to life these momentous historical events, and his role and stature as an exemplar of a heroic era of our national movement. Interspersed with this main narrative are some interesting accounts that bring into focus the other side of Abid Hasan Safrani—his lighter moments when he breaks out into laughter while relating funny events in his life.

But what should make the book of further interest is its delineation of Safrani's life after his INA days. In his later life, he emerged as an outstanding diplomat, playing a major role on several occasions in India's relations with foreign powers. Descriptions of key episodes from this eventful and exciting period of his career should be of immense value and interest to those engaged in researching India's foreign policy and diplomacy.

It is the chapters written by the above-mentioned three authors, articles collected from various sources, reminiscences of family and friends, and tributes paid by admirers, and notes left behind by Safrani himself which were woven together to form the book. In acknowledgment, mention must be made of the Delhi-based journal *Mainstream*, the Netaji Research Bureau of Kolkata, and the freelance journalist Geeta Doctor, who all willingly granted permission to reproduce their articles. It is hoped that this book will help readers rediscover a hero of our national movement, and also get a better understanding of the evolution of a new and independent India.

Sumanta Banerjee
October 2021

ACKNOWLEDGEMENTS

The authors would like to thank all the friends and family members who contributed to this effort by fondly recalling their memories of Manna, Abid Hasan Safrani.

The contribution of C. Narendra Reddy was tremendous in terms of researching and helping to put together many of the chapters.

A special thanks to Sugata Bose for his encouragement and for writing a wonderful 'Foreword'.

Sugata Bose, the Netaji Research Bureau, Kolkata, Geeta Doctor, Sumit Chakravarty of *Mainstream Weekly*, and Ravindra Kumar of *The Statesman* promptly granted permissions to reproduce extracts from their respective writings and publications.

Thanks are also due to Sumanta Banerjee, who wrote the 'Preface', Majaz Panjetan, for his valuable suggestions, Bizeth Banerjee and others for their assistance at various stages of compiling this book.

The authors greatly missed the presence of the late Anwar Ali Khan, who was close to Abid Hasan Safrani and could have contributed tremendously.

Finally, a grateful thank you to Sajid Mahmood for carefully reading and editing the manuscript.

1 ABID HASAN SAFRANI

An Outstanding Indian Patriot of Hyderabad

This is the story of a valiant patriot and freedom fighter of India—Abid Hasan Safrani. He was Netaji Subhas Chandra Bose's close confidant and constant companion from his days in Germany, to the years of the Indian National Army (INA). Safrani was Netaji's sole co-traveller on his daring and historic submarine journey from Germany to Japan during the height of World War II. He is credited with coining the salutation 'Jai Hind' for the INA. After Independence, 'Jai Hind' was adopted as the official salutation of the Indian Army and the country in general.

Born in Hyderabad on 11 April 1911 to Tehsildar Amir Hasan and Fakhrul Hajia Begum, a lady of Persian origin, he was named Zain-ul-Abdin Hasan. He grew up in an environment that laid emphasis on patriotism, personal integrity and creativity. The study of both sciences and humanities was encouraged to gain a holistic view. His schooling was at the much sought-after St George's Grammar School of Hyderabad. He had a strong inclination towards mathematics at school in which he always scored the highest.

After finishing school, Abid Hasan joined Nizam College, but left it soon to answer Mahatma Gandhi's call to join the struggle for freedom. He joined the Congress Volunteer Corps in Bombay. As there was not much work there, he followed his brothers and joined Gandhiji's Sabarmati Ashram in Ahmedabad.

At the Ashram, Abid Hasan was assigned to the Udyog Mandir to learn card weaving of khadi. During the learning process he was informed that one of the organisers of the planned Dandi March, Kharak Bahadur Singh of Rohtak, was looking for Muslim volunteers. Abid Hasan immediately left for Rohtak, only to discover that the team had already proceeded to Ahmedabad. He returned to Ahmedabad where he came to know that the team had been arrested. Having missed being part of the Dandi March, he resumed his course of card weaving at the Sabarmati Ashram.

At Sabarmati he dutifully followed the protocol of cleaning toilets, sweeping and doing sundry menial tasks. The stay at the Ashram played a key role in his personal development and influenced his future life. It instilled in him a strong sense of patriotism along with humility. Later in life, Abid Hasan recalled the salt-less meals and how the discipline of the Ashram led to camaraderie and togetherness amongst its inmates as it did not take into account lineage, religion, caste or area of origin of individuals.

On leaving the Ashram, Abid Hasan joined a group in Bombay that was planning to raid the Nasik distillery in support of the anti-liquor movement. As a cover he joined Navjivan Trust that promoted Gandhian thought. The Police Intelligence Cell discovered the plot. Abid Hasan and the group were arrested and charged with sedition. He was sentenced to six month's rigorous imprisonment. Fortunately, he was released early as part of the Gandhi-Irwin Pact of 1931.

In 1935, instead of going to England for higher studies, as was the convention in those days, Abid Hasan went to Berlin to pursue engineering as per the desire of his mother, Ammajan. Ammajan was at the forefront of the freedom struggle, and did not want anything to do with the British. In Berlin he met Netaji Subhas Chandra Bose, whose call to join the freedom struggle was so strong that Abid Hasan promptly left his course without finishing it and joined Netaji as his personal secretary and interpreter.

The Germans handed over the captured Indian soldiers fighting for the British to Netaji. Netaji used these liberated prisoners of war to raise the Free India Legion. At the Legion, they often discussed their future plans for India. One such discussion was about what the flag of independent India would look like. Belonging to different religions, they discussed this in a spirit of accommodation, agreeing to a design that featured each representative colour in equal width.

Another issue that arose was the need for a common salutation that was essential for maintaining the discipline of the Army. The soldiers, who felt betrayed by the British, did not want to use English salutations. An alternative had to be found, and Safrani was entrusted with this task. Initially he proposed 'Hello'. Netaji was far from impressed and rejected it outright. Safrani's next proposal was 'Jai Hindustan Ki'. Netaji found this interesting but too long. Finally, 'Jai Hind' was agreed upon. It became the official salutation of the INA when Netaji took over as its leader. Post-Independence, 'Jai Hind' was declared the salutation of the Indian Army and government employees. Pandit Jawaharlal Nehru, the first prime minister of independent India, asked people to repeat 'Jai Hind' after him, three times, at the end of his first Independence Day speech from the ramparts of the Red Fort. Since then this practice has been followed by all prime ministers of India till date.

With the German slowdown on their eastern front, Netaji decided to shift base to Japanese territory, closer to India. Safrani was Netaji's sole companion on his historic journey, by German and Japanese submarines from Kiel in Germany to Japanese territory in Malaysia. They started their journey in a German submarine and switched to a Japanese one in choppy waters off the coast of Madagascar. This was later recorded as the first inter-submarine transfer on the high seas.

On reaching Singapore, with Safrani by his side, Netaji took over the INA. The INA had been formed by the Japanese intelligence unit on the same pattern as Netaji's Free India Legion of Germany, using captured Indian prisoners of war.

Safrani was constantly with the INA, fighting from Burma to Imphal in India. This fierce battle has been recorded by him in his article 'Our Men in Imphal'. With the tide turning in favour of the Allies, the INA started losing and was finally defeated. At the fag-end of the war, while accompanying Netaji from Singapore to Tokyo, Abid Hasan was asked to disembark in Saigon and return to Hanoi. On reaching there, he was captured by the British and imprisoned.

A number of INA officers were put on trial in Delhi after the war. There was a public outcry against these trials as people considered them to be freedom fighters and not war criminals. The trial ended, acquitting most of them. Safrani was released from Singapore jail and returned to India as it neared independence.

In post-Independence India, Nehru inducted Safrani into the Indian Foreign Service. He was posted to several countries including Egypt, China, Switzerland, Iraq, Syria, Senegal and Denmark. Safrani's dispatches from Iraq, in which he gave very accurate reports of the impending revolution there, were highly appreciated and Nehru formally acknowledged this in Parliament.

Abid Hasan Safrani settled on a farm of Shaikhpet in Toli Chowki near Golconda, Hyderabad, spending his last days farming and living a quiet, ordinary life. Little did his neighbours know that they were living next to an individual who had played such an important role in the history of the Indian freedom struggle. He passed away peacefully in 1984.

Jai Hind!

Abid Hasan belonged to the state of Hyderabad that was ruled by the Asaf Jahi dynasty till Independence. The seventh and the last Nizam, Osman Ali Khan Asif Jah VII, ran his administration with skilled professionals, selected regardless of their religion, caste or region. This is best illustrated by certain events at the time of Independence. When the departure plans of the British were being worked out, the Nizam did not send his representatives to the Constituent Assembly of either India or Pakistan. He gave his reasons in the firman issued on 11 June 1947 in which he rejected the communal division of India. The firman read:

> In my State, the two major communities live side by side and I have sought, since I became ruler, to promote by every means, good and friendly relations between them. My ancestors and I always regarded the Muslims and the Hindus as the two eyes of the State, and the State itself to be the indivisible asset of all the communities inhabiting it.[1]

The Nizam's nonpartisan approach in governance resulted in extensive development. Under able prime ministers like Salar Jung I, Maharaja Kishan Pershad and Sir Akbar Hydari, education in the state was revamped to modern times and institutions like the Osmania University were set up. The state of Hyderabad made great strides in medicine, engineering, and water management. It stood out among the princely states with its own currency, postal system, railways and airways.

People were happy with this approach and development, but there were some murmurs of discontent as well. Resentment against the Nizam and his autocratic ways was growing among informed sections of Hindus and Muslims. Hyderabad's youth studying in other states of India saw the tide turning against

British rule. Those studying in England were exposed to the concept and functioning of Western democracies. They started thinking in terms of implementing changes to introduce popular democracy in their own state as well.

Playing upon this feeling, Mohammed Ali Jinnah felt that he could extend his influence in the region. He visited the state of Hyderabad a couple of times for this purpose, but to no avail. His first visit in April 1919 was in connection with a legal case as a lawyer. Some elite of Hyderabad asked him to give a lecture on 'The India of Today'. At that time there were agitations taking place in British India against the Rowlatt Act. Not wanting to aggravate the situation further, the Nizam's administration advised Jinnah to decline addressing that meeting. Ignoring the advice, Jinnah went ahead and addressed the meeting. His speech in fact compared the Hyderabad States favourably with British India. The Executive Council of the Nizam issued an order on 18 April 1919, on Jinnah's return to Bombay, telling him 'not to visit any part of His Exalted Highness's Dominions on any account whatsoever, professional or otherwise, without permission from H.E.H'.[2] The order was withdrawn much later in 1930.

The purpose of Jinnah's visit in 1946 was to oppose the appointment of Sir Mirza Ismail as President of the Nizam's Executive Council. Sir Mirza Ismail was known as an able administrator. His tenure as Dewan of Mysore was testimony of that. The appointment was, however, opposed by the Ittehadul-Muslimeen, an extreme Right-wing party. In this connection, Jinnah sought an appointment with the Nizam.

It is said that Jinnah entered the room smoking a cigar and seated himself in front of the Nizam, with his legs outstretched. The outraged Nizam said in a high-pitched voice: 'Is this the way you behave towards the Nizam of Hyderabad?'[3]

Jinnah immediately withdrew his legs and discarded his cigar, apologising.

The Nizam continued: 'I do not want any outside interference in my affairs. I can take care of the interests of my own people. I do not wish to discuss the matter with you.'[4]

Jinnah was summarily dismissed. The incident was a reaffirmation of the Nizam's cosmopolitan approach that attracted people from all over India and foreign lands.

This environment left a deep impression on Abid Hasan's thinking and perspective.

NOTES

1. M. A. Nayeem, *The Splendour of Hyderabad: The Last Phase of an Oriental Culture, 1591–1948 A.D.* (Jaico Publishing House, 1987), 57.
2. N. Ramesan, ed. *The Freedom Struggle in Hyderabad, Vol. IV, 1921–1947* (Hyderabad: Hyderabad State Committee Appointed for the Compilation of the History of the Freedom Movement in Hyderabad, 1966), 10.
3. Ibid.
4. Ibid.

3 ROOTS OF THE FREEDOM STRUGGLE IN HYDERABAD

The early roots of the freedom struggle can be traced back to times when Sir Mir Turab Ali Khan, Salar Jung I became the Prime Minister of Hyderabad in 1853. At the outbreak of the Rebellion of 1857, he supported the British. Except for an attack on the British Residency by private, intrepid and courageous revolutionaries, the Hyderabad contingent remained loyal. With the British preoccupied with the rebellion, Salar Jung I pushed a lot of reforms. These included starting postal services, establishing a court of justice, reorganising the police force, internal railways, opening the rail link to Bombay, modernisation of education and promoting a free press. Above all, he improved the finances of Hyderabad State.

All these activities prompted the Viceroy of India, Lord Robert Bulwer Lytton to state in one of his communications to the Hyderabad Resident Richard Meade, 'The intrigues of Salar Jung were regarded by me as the greatest danger to which the British power in India was exposed during my Viceroyalty—a danger far greater than any which was involved in war or famine.'[1] Fearing the awakening that these reforms could bring, the British created such difficult situations that Salar Jung I was forced to submit his resignation. The Nizam persuaded him to withdraw it.

The modernisation of education and promotion of a free press laid the base of broader social movements. As these social movements grew, they started integrating with the national freedom movement. The path taken by the social reformer and educationist Aghornath Chattopadhyay is an example.

Aghornath Chattopadhyay was the first Indian to get a Ph.D. in science from the Edinburgh University. Salar Jung I invited him as part of his process of modernising the education system. Chattopadhyay came to Hyderabad in 1878 to start an English-medium school and later, the Hyderabad College that came to be known as the Nizam College. Unlike most government officials, who were usually known to live secluded lives, he soon became a well-known figure in social and political circles of Hyderabad. Chattopadhyay's house became a hub of several movements.

The political awakening of the people of Hyderabad began when in 1883 they started agitating against the Nizam government's Chanda Railway line project linking Hyderabad with Warangal. They felt it was being built not for public welfare but to tap the Godavari Valley Coalfield for commercial purposes. The laying of the line would disrupt life in many villages. This was the first time that the people of Hyderabad had opposed and questioned the Nizam's government. The British, still shaken by the Revolt of 1857, were worried.

Dr Aghornath Chattopadhyay supported the Chanda agitation openly. On 20 May 1883,[2] while he was discussing the Chanda Railway agitation with some prominent citizens at his house, a police contingent suddenly arrived without warning and whisked him away. He was taken to the railway station, put into a lower-class compartment and shunted out of the state. He was also suspended from service. The event became the talk of the town. This could happen only with the orders of the highest authority, namely the Nizam or the British Resident. All the evidence suggested that it was the British Resident who was responsible.

Dr Chattopadhyay's dismissal and expulsion from the state happened soon after the death of Salar Jung I in February the same year. It was not only because he was a protégé of Salar Jung, but mainly because of his active involvement in various social and political movements that popular protests in the state against his expulsion spread nationwide. His deportation and expulsion created intense resentment amongst the people towards the British authorities. The Bombay print media like *The Times of India* and *The Englishman* covered it prominently. Seeing the rapidly rising public discontent, the Viceroy intervened and lifted the orders barring Dr Chattopadhyay from entering Hyderabad. He was also reinstated as principal of the Nizam College.

Dr Aghornath Chattopadhyay returned with stronger conviction and resolve. When the Congress Party was founded in December 1885, he joined it along with other leading public figures of Hyderabad like Mulla Abdul Qayum, Ramachandra Pillai and Mohib Hussain. In a way, the expulsion of Dr Chattopadhyay backfired for the authorities—it only ended up inflaming popular agitations instead of suppressing them. As people across the country started joining the Congress en masse, simultaneously the process of integrating various regional social and cultural movements into the national freedom struggle also started. Young women like Begum Amir Hasan and Sarojini Chattopadhyay were witnessing all these tumultuous events, the fervour of nationalism slowly taking root in their hearts.

Those who joined the Congress started the process of inculcating nationalistic feelings among the educated and attracting the masses to the movement. This was supported by an explosion in newspapers and weeklies. Thanks to the encouraging policies of Salar Jung I, by 1900 several of these had started publishing. Prominent among them in English were the *Hyderabad Telegraph*, *Deccan Standard*, *Deccan Times*, *Hyderabad Chronicle*, *Gulbarga Samachar* and *Champavati* in Marathi, *Dina Vartamana* in Telugu, *Shaukat ul Islam* in Urdu, and *Hazar Dastan* in Sindhi.

The Congress opened its Hyderabad chapter in 1918. To begin with, it limited its activities to the promotion of khadi and the upliftment of backward castes. The Hyderabad State Congress started becoming politically active in the 1930s. A state conference was planned for 9 September 1938 under the leadership of Pandit Govinda Rao Nanal.

The Nizam's government, being closely allied to the British, banned the State Congress altogether. As the Congress was opposed to the Muslim fundamentalist party Majlis-e-Ittehad-ul-Muslimeen (MIM), the Nizam's administration, under pressure of the MIM, declared the Congress a communal party. The declaration banning the Congress stated: 'His Exalted Highness' Government has no objection to the establishment of political organisations in the State provided that these are on a strictly non-communal basis and have no affiliations outside the State.'[3]

The State Congress Action Committee reiterated that it was the birthright of the people to organise political associations. They did not bear any hatred or malice towards any community or individual. They were second to none in their loyalty to the Nizam and the country, but they wanted to live as self-respecting and free citizens.

The Action Committee declared that the ban on the formation of the Hyderabad State Congress would be defied by a satyagraha which would be individual in character; the people were told not to hold any public meetings and demonstrations for the present. To absolve ordinary members from responsibility their primary membership of the State Congress was suspended. Nothing contrary to the creed of nonviolence and truth was to be done as these were the sheet-anchors of the State Congress. Satyagrahis were advised to inform the police of the place and time of the satyagrah that they proposed to perform.

Despite these assurances, the state police arrested the Congress Working Committee members. The reason given was that the Congress Action Committee aimed at interfering with the administration of the state and that its activities were subversive of the maintenance of law and order. Furthermore, its very existence would be dangerous to peace and harmonious relations between the various communities in the state.

With the Congress Working Committee under arrest, Swami Ramananda Tirth took charge and launched satyagraha in Hyderabad City on 27 October 1928. As per the directions laid down by the Working Committee earlier, prior intimation was given to the Police Commissioner of Hyderabad. As the satyagraha started, Swami Tirth was arrested.

The satyagraha was stopped on 24 December 1938 on the call of Gandhi, who asked Sir Akbar Hyderi, the Prime Minister of Hyderabad, to lift the ban on Congress. Sir Hyderi did not agree to this, but released the Congress leaders after banning them from the State of Hyderabad. While the Congress was denied primary civil rights, the communal organisation Majlis-e-Ittehad-ul-Muslimeen was permitted to carry on with its activities and play key roles in the Nizam's administration. Ultimately, the MIM was instrumental in the downfall of the Nizam. Swami Ramananda Tirth was finally released in mid-February 1939. He continued to play an active role in the freedom movement.

When Gandhi started the Quit India Movement in 1942, Swami Tirth wrote to the Congress leaders about Gandhi's call to 'Do or Die'. He wrote to the Nizam of Hyderabad, demanding the lifting of the ban on Congress. After the Bombay session of the Congress in August 1942, Swami Tirth returned to Hyderabad, only to be arrested at the railway station. People in Hyderabad responded to the 'Do or Die' call in large numbers. Many gave up their government jobs and joined the freedom movement. The government came down heavily on them, arresting them on various charges. Those arrested included Padmaja Naidu, Harishchandra Heda, G. S. Melkote among many others. The increasing pressure forced the government to lift the ban on Congress in April 1946.

Apart from the non-cooperation movement, other ideas and programmes of Gandhi like boycotting foreign goods and promoting khadi caught the imagination of people all over India, giving the Congress a formidable mass base. The British began to see the writing on the wall. Gandhiji on his part did not lose patience and continued his non-violent struggle.

Subhas Chandra Bose and Abid Hasan opted for a different line, deciding to take the mighty British Empire head on. They raised the INA with the help of the Axis Powers (Germany, Italy and Japan) during World War II and fought battles to gain freedom. Although they lost the battles on the ground, their brave fight compelled the British to hasten their exit from India. Many British officers, army men and political leaders have stated in their memoirs that the activities of the INA were a crucial factor that influenced the British decision to leave India.

NOTES

1. *The Freedom Struggle in Hyderabad, Vol. II, 1857–1885* (Hyderabad: Hyderabad State Committee Appointed for the Compilation of the History of the Freedom Movement in Hyderabad, 1956), 257.

2. Ibid., 291.

3. N. Ramesan, ed. *The Freedom Struggle in Hyderabad, Vol. IV, 1921–1947* (Hyderabad: Hyderabad State Committee Appointed for the Compilation of the History of the Freedom Movement in Hyderabad, 1966), 185.

4 THE PIONEERING WOMEN OF HYDERABAD

The story of Hyderabadi freedom fighters is not complete without an account of the central role played by the women of Hyderabad. The Nizam of Hyderabad, Osman Ali Khan led the way in liberating them from the shackles of tradition. Apart from starting schools and colleges for girls, he brought the women of his own court out of purdah, thus setting an example for others to follow. These efforts at reform were instrumental in spreading modern education and thinking amongst women, and many rose in their turn to spread it amongst their peers.

Towering above the others were the twentieth-century pioneers Sughra Humayun Mirza and Tayyaba Begum Bilgrami. Both these women made significant strides towards the social upliftment of Hyderabad's girls by making school and college education accessible to them. The Safdariya Girls High School founded by Sughra Humayun Mirza and Tayyaba Begum's Anjumane Khawatin School are still running strong. The winds of education and social reform were travelling fast, and literary discussions were springing up outside of formal institutions too. Jamalunissa Begum Baji's salon, for instance, was unique for the haven it provided for Leftists and progressive intellectuals of the Hyderabad State.

Fakhrul Hajia Begum, Abid Hasan's mother, who had hitherto been confined to the domestic sphere, played a crucial role in raising national consciousness amongst women.

Fakhrul Hajia Begum was born to Persian parents in 1870. They moved from Bombay to Hyderabad when her father was appointed as calligrapher at the Government Printing Press. Outgoing and friendly at school, two of her classmates thought Fakhrul would make a suitable partner to their father, who had lost his wife. The same age as them, they also thought Fakhrul would make for good company. Fakhrul Hajia thus became the third wife of Talukdar Amir Hasan.

Fakhrul Hajia and Amir Hasan had fourteen children. Though Persian by birth, she imbibed the syncretic culture of Hyderabad and became thoroughly Indianised of her own accord. She shed her burqa and took to wearing a sari, as seen in all her photographs. Apart from her mother tongue Farsi, her home language Urdu, English and a smattering of French, she also spoke several other Indian languages. As her husband was the district collector for several areas, the family travelled a lot, and Fakhrul picked up the regional languages along the way. She was often heard singing happily to herself in Marathi, Telugu or Kannada while grinding flour in the chakki.

Amir Hasan was known to be scholarly, introverted and a loyal civil servant. Fakhrul Hajia, however, was a strong-headed, strong-willed person, and often had views opposing those of her husband. She also had an open and sharp mind, and harboured virtually no prejudice. And she had a big say in the upbringing of her children. Most well-to-do Hyderabadi families at the time preferred to send their boys to Oxford, Cambridge or law schools in England for higher education and to prepare them for the Civil Service Examinations. Overruling her husband, Fakhrul Hajia sent her children to Germany instead. Her eldest son, Mehdi Hasan, took his Ph.D. from Leipzig, Jafar from Heidelburg, and Abid joined the Technische Hochschule for Engineering in Berlin. Khurshid had no choice but to come away when the war broke out.

During her educational years, Fakhrul Hajia made the acquaintance of Sarojini Chattopadhyay, who lived next door, in the house called 'Golden Threshold'. Daughter of Aghornath Chattopadhyay, vivacious and extremely intelligent, Sarojini was nine years younger than Fakhrul. The two grew close and became lifelong friends. Sarojini (later, Naidu) was an integral part of the Hasan family. Sarojini and her daughter Padmaja maintained strong relationships with Fakhrul Hajia, until their deaths.

Sarojini cogently articulated the need for righting the wrongs heaped on India by the British. She encouraged women all over the country to get actively involved in Gandhi's 'non-cooperation' movement. She told them to be fearless in exercising their will and to fight tyranny in any form—homegrown or external. With her natural leadership, strong sense of justice and powerful oratory, young Sarojini soon became the feminine face of India's struggle for freedom, and part of the inner circle of Gokhale and Gandhi. It was inevitable that her patriotism and politics would influence her friends and peers. Fakhrul was deeply inspired by Sarojini, who emerged as one of the most prominent women nationalists in the Indian freedom struggle led by Gandhiji.

The country was going through a tremendous upheaval, with nationalists wanting to overthrow the British yoke. At a time that many Hyderabadis, particularly the aristocracy, wished to remain loyal to the British, Fakhrul Hajia's pro-nationalist views were very strong and clear-sighted. As her involvement in the national movement increased, she switched over to wearing plain khadi saris and made her sons wear khadi clothes and caps. Her sons, who were already exposed to liberal ideas in Europe, readily took to the idealism of the then rising national leaders. When Gandhi's call came to boycott British goods, the Hasan family was among the very first to respond.

Fakhrul the matriarch acted with zeal. Along with her sons and daughters, she went about Hyderabad asking neighbours and friends to part with whatever they could of their British clothes and expensive imported accessories. All these were brought and piled up in the grounds of her home 'Abid Manzil'. The collection soon grew into a hill. With a British formal hat and a British-made walking stick perched right on top, the pile was then set ablaze, marking 1925 as one of the most momentous years in Fakhrul's life. Several prominent citizens of Hyderabad came to witness the bonfire.

High up in the Residency, the British Resident of Hyderabad saw the flames, and was incensed when he learnt of the huge bonfire at Abid Manzil that had become the talk of the town. He summoned Amir Hasan, who worked for the Nizam's government, rebuked him, told him to stop this nonsense at once and ensure that no such activity was repeated.

Amir Hasan returned home and told his wife about the Resident's reprimand, asking her to 'Please restrain the children'. Fakhrul responded by saying, 'Sarkar, this is my house. My father gave it to me. And my children are free to do as they please.' Her strong, albeit brusque words are a family lore to this day.

Fakhrul Hajia (Begum Amir Hasan) came to be universally known as 'Ammajan'. Even leaders of the stature of Mahatma Gandhi, Jawaharlal Nehru, Subhas Chandra Bose, Abul Kalam Azad and Zakir Husain knew her by that name.

Ammajan schooled her children thoroughly in the national politics of the time. The first of the children to join Mahatma Gandhi's Ashram was Badrul Hasan. Impressed by his flair for writing, Gandhiji appointed him the editor of his weekly *Young India* in 1925. Among the notable books Badrul Hasan wrote during this period was *Evils of Drug and Alcohol in India* (Madras, 1925), which has a long preface by Gandhiji. Badrul was hounded by pro-British fanatic Muslims, who threatened to kill him and throw his body into the river. It is said that whenever Badrul visited Sabarmati Ashram, Gandhiji would send his secretary Pyarelal to personally receive and send him off safely at the railway station.

Badrul Hasan was considered the genius of the family. An astute entrepreneur, he was instrumental in the revival of several cottage industries like bidri, Karimnagar silver filigree and Siddipet silk, and a founding member of the Hyderabad Co-operative Society and the Hyderabad Cottage Industry. Known to be a voracious reader, Badrul became an agent of the Oxford University Press in India. He founded the Hyderabad Book Depot at Abid Road, which remained the leading bookstore of Hyderabad for forty years, from 1920 to early 1960. Badrul Hasan's life and work left a deep influence on Abid Hasan's thinking.

In their turn, Badrul's brothers, Jafar and Abid Hasan, also joined Gandhiji's Ashram. They would later recall the strict discipline, the communal work shared by all, the salt-less meals, all taken in a spirit of togetherness. They wore khadi when their friends wore fine clothes, and led spartan lives while others lived lavishly. Each of the brothers courted arrest in response to Gandhi's call for non-cooperation and satyagraha, and spent varying terms in jail. Abid Hasan would recall that when he was released from Arthur Road Jail in Bombay, and the family went to receive him, he wanted to run towards them, but couldn't; his legs had no strength left from being confined to a cell.

As the freedom struggle grew more intense, Ammajan took part in many All India Women's Conferences, travelling across the country to cities far from home, addressing gatherings, urging women to join the national movement in large numbers along with the men. She also played an important role as a spokeswoman for Muslim women.

When Partition was officially announced in 1946, Ammajan was in Lucknow, and according to her granddaughter Mahpara Husain, she went to meet Mahatma Gandhi by special appointment in Delhi, and she protested at the partition looming dark over the nation. Gandhi reportedly told her not to blame him, but to 'blame her children', by which he evidently meant the people of India and Pakistan, and that he had been compelled to accept the Partition against his wishes.

5 GANDHI, BOSE AND ABID HASAN

The great poet Rabindranath Tagore gave the sobriquets of 'Mahatma' or Great Soul to Gandhi and 'Netaji' or Revered Leader to Subhas Bose. These sobriquets stuck to them like garlands. Gandhi and Bose were both strong leaders. Their approach and attitude differed, but their goal was common: a free India.

Similarly, the suffix 'Safrani' adopted by Abid Hasan is derived from the word for saffron, a colour associated with sacrifice in the Indian subcontinent. In ancient Indian philosophy, the concept of sacrifice meant overcoming all desires to attain salvation. For Abid Hasan, it meant giving up everything for the sake of winning freedom for his country.

By the early 1920s Gandhi had become the leading figure of the Congress Party and had succeeded in making it into a mass organisation. His nationwide call for civil disobedience and non-cooperation had brought thousands of people under the fold of the Congress.

The Indian farmer, despite suffering oppression for centuries and being driven to hard times, and also because of it, had developed a keen sense of survival. Gandhi developed that same survival instinct which gave him an edge over other leaders. He was practical and stuck to his mission. The four cardinal facts that he kept in mind while leading the national freedom movement were:

1. The masses were afraid to face the baton and of going to prison. Gandhi's primary objective was to free them of these fears.
2. The oppressed classes who ran into millions were not organised.

3. Various governments had divided the people along lines of religion, region, caste and creed. Gandhi saw the pressing need to unite them.
4. Poverty and unemployment had depressed and weakened the masses. Their economic self-sufficiency was an urgent necessity before any fighting spirit could be kindled in them.

In 1921, Subhas Chandra Bose gave up the idea of joining the Indian Civil Service even after qualifying. He returned to India to join Gandhi, with whom he worked closely for over twelve years. He faithfully followed Gandhi's nonviolent struggle. Over a period, he started getting disillusioned with the slow progress of the freedom struggle and felt that more radical and militant strategies were required. The hangings of Bhagat Singh, Sukhdev Thapar and Shivaram Rajguru in 1931 disturbed Bose profoundly, provoking him to deliver a fiery speech at the Karachi Session of the Congress. He urged people to emulate Bhagat Singh. Bose was taken into custody and imprisoned.

Lord Willingdon who replaced Lord Irwin as Viceroy was a hardliner. He abrogated the Gandhi-Irwin Pact and suppressed civil liberties, including freedom of speech and assembly. Gandhi boycotted the Round Table Conference held in November 1931. One of the reasons quoted was the British Government's refusal to let Subhas Bose be part of the Indian team.

In prison Bose fell extremely ill. His deteriorating condition forced the British to release him in February 1933 on the condition that he leave the country. He sailed to Europe where he first spent time in a sanatorium for medical treatment. On his recovery, Bose shifted to Berlin in July 1933.

Despite persisting health issues, Bose visited several European countries including Czechoslovakia and Poland as an unofficial ambassador of India's freedom struggle. He met leaders of all shades of political opinion, from fascist to communists. His basic purpose was to seek support for India's freedom from British control. This was also the period that saw Bose's transformation from a leader to a statesman.[1]

In Vienna he met Vithalbhai Patel (elder brother of Sardar Patel), a freedom fighter and a critic of Gandhi's often conciliatory policy. On 9 May 1933, the two leaders issued a statement from Vienna stating that: 'We are clearly of the opinion that as a political leader Mahatma Gandhi has not succeeded. Non-cooperation cannot be abandoned, but the form of non-cooperation must be changed into a militant one and there must be freedom for a fight to be waged on all fronts.'[2] This came to be known as the 'Bose-Patel Manifesto'.

While in Europe, Bose researched and wrote the first part of his book *The Indian Struggle 1920–1942*, a detailed study of the Indian freedom movement between the decades 1920 and 1942. He also increased his contact with Indian students and the youth to get them involved in India's independence movement.

As for Abid Hasan, he went to Berlin in 1935 to study engineering. When he read in the newspapers that Subhas Bose was in Berlin, he went to see him along with his friend Swami. Abid Hasan too was disillusioned by the British tactics of delaying India's independence, by the increasing repression and imposition of arbitrary laws that further restricted basic civil rights and freedoms of Indians. Both Abid and Swami offered their services to Bose. They were given some 'clerical jobs' as Abid Hasan mentions in his notes that: 'Subhas Babu was so busy, and it was no use hanging around him. We would go and just give *haziri*.'[3] That was their first contact with Subhas Bose.

Meanwhile, Bose was growing increasingly discontented with Germany for its selfish, narrow-minded and arrogant pursuit of its interests. Nehru persuaded him to return to India. Bose returned to India in March 1936. His dynamism led him to be elected as the youngest president of the Congress Party in January 1938. During his tenure, differences emerged between him and Gandhi. The direction that Bose wanted the Congress to take was not aligned with Gandhi's thinking. Due to these differences Gandhi was not in favour of a second term for Bose and supported Pattabhi Sitaramayya for the Congress presidentship. However, despite this, Bose was re-elected as President of the Indian National Congress. Gandhi was unhappy with Bose's re-election and treated

Sitaramayya's defeat as his own. Seeing Gandhi's disappointment, thirteen members of the Congress Working Committee resigned. With the growing schism within the party and the Gandhi faction's hostility towards him, it became increasingly difficult for Bose to work as the president, and he resigned from the Congress presidentship in 1939.

In August of the same year, Bose was removed from the Presidentship of Bengal's Provincial Congress Committee for his utterances and suspended for three years on charges of violating party discipline. Freed from the limitations of party politics, Bose went in for an open challenge to British rule. On 19 March 1940, Bose presided over the All-India Anti-Compromise Conference at Ramgarh in Bihar, organised by Swami Sahajanand Saraswati, where he expressed his anguish at the compromising nature of the Congress, and said that Gandhiji left for Shimla as soon as World War I broke out and, without consulting the Congress Working Committee, informed the Viceroy that he was in favour of India rendering unconditional help to Great Britain in the war.

Bose was arrested on 2 July 1940. He went on a hunger strike in captivity, which forced the authorities to release him in November 1940; all this while he continued to urge the Congress to launch national civil disobedience. On 20 May 1940, Nehru made a statement that, 'Launching a civil disobedience campaign at a time when Britain is engaged in a life and death struggle would be an act derogatory to India's honour.'[4] Gandhi also said that he did not want to win independence from the ruins of Britain. Bose, on the other hand, saw the war as a golden opportunity to win freedom by joining hands with Germany. Gandhi disagreed and, in his written reply on 29 December 1940 from Sevagram, Wardha, told Bose: 'till one of us is converted to the other's view, we must sail in different boats, though their destination may appear, only appear to be the same.'[5]

Due to his ill health Bose had been permitted to stay at home in Calcutta under house arrest. He escaped in disguise from India and made his way to Berlin. His arduous journey took nearly two and a half months as he travelled incognito by road, rail and air through Afghanistan and Russia. He was tailed by British agents who had been ordered to assassinate him on the direct orders of Prime Minister Winston Churchill. Bose reached Berlin on 28 March 1941.

In Berlin, Subhas Bose initially stayed under the assumed name of Orlando Mazzotta with an Italian passport. After several months of waiting and quiet negotiations, the German authorities finally agreed to help him form a small army called 'The Indian Legion'. The battalions comprised Indian soldiers of the British army captured as prisoners of war by the Germans. They also helped him set up the *Azad Hind Radio* in Berlin. A three-storey building in Lichtenstein Allee became the office of the Free India Centre called *The Centrale.*

Abid Hasan stayed back in Germany when the war started as he wanted to complete his engineering studies. To finance his studies, he had joined the German Radio as a translator.

NOTES

1. Bhuvan Lall, *The Man India Missed the Most: Subhas Chandra Bose* (Chennai: Notion Press, 2017), 116.
2. Sugata Bose, *His Majesty's Opponent: Subhas Chandra Bose and India's Struggle against Empire* (New Delhi: Penguin Books India, 2013), 87.
3. Abid Hasan, 'A Soldier Remembers', *The Oracle* 6(1) (January 1984): 27.
4. Felix Morrow, 'To the Workers and Peasants of India: Manifesto of the Fourth International', *Fourth International* 3(10) (September 1942): 296–301. Available at https://www.marxists.org/history/etol/document/fi/1938-1949/ww/1942-ww03.htm (accessed 12 September 2022).
5. Gandhi quoted in Lall, *The Man India Missed the Most*, 164.

6 WITH SUBHASBABU IN GERMANY[1]

Abid Hasan met Subhas Chandra Bose again in November 1941. One day his friend N. G. Swami told him about an Italian gentleman by the name of Mr. Orlando Mazzotta who often talked about India. He said it would be interesting to meet him. Swami took him to a building in Lichtenstein Allee to meet Mr. Mazzotta. Swami went to some other office and asked Abid to go and meet the gentleman. As he approached the gentleman, who was sitting in a large office, Abid gasped 'Subhasbabu!'. There was a pause of a couple of minutes. Subhas Bose led Abid Hasan to a sofa and asked him to sit down. He ordered for a pot of tea. When it came, he made a cup of tea and gave it to Abid Hasan. Bose spoke of irrelevant matters to let Abid relax and get over his surprise.

Then he asked Abid Hasan, 'What do you think of the Indian situation?' to which Abid could only respond with 'Sir!'

Bose then asked Abid Hasan about his joining the Congress, visiting the Sabarmati Ashram and then going to jail. And, having gone through all this, his reasons for leaving the freedom movement.

Abid Hasan responded, 'Sir, to be very frank, I don't believe in Gandhiji's leadership anymore, because I had left my studies on the understanding that the fight would be a fight till the end. But in between, the Gandhi-Irwin Pact came, and I remember leaving the jail in tears. Now, I don't want to do anything halfway. I find that every leader in the Congress is a qualified person. They have other means of subsistence. I cannot join the Congress Party and go about with a begging bowl! So I had to get myself qualified. That was the main reason I stayed back in Germany when the war started.'

Taking his assent for granted, Bose then told Abid Hasan that he was now part of his team. Hasan asked, 'Sir, when do I start?

Should I resign from the radio?' 'Immediately!' said Bose. Abid Hasan joined the very next day.

If one trait defined Abid Hasan most it was the spirit of sacrifice, and this is best shown by the circumstances in which he joined the Azad Hind Fauj when Netaji bid him join. Abid Hasan said he had only one semester left to finish his course and that he could join Netaji after the finals. His family had sent him to study bearing great hardships; how could he return now without qualifying?

Netaji was furious and said, 'I do not need selfish people like you. The country needs you now—not after you have qualified.'

Abid Hasan recalls that he tossed and turned the whole night before finally deciding to leave his studies and join the freedom struggle under Netaji. He never regretted the decision.

To begin with, the team had very few members. They were not more than six or seven, but they had started the Azad Hind Radio on short wave, aiming their broadcasts at the Indian population. The question of military organisation had arisen and was being discussed.

Bose shared with them his account of joining and leaving the Congress. How he got arrested, escaped, and travelled halfway around the world to reach Germany. He told them what he had thought out and planned when he was in jail. His plan was to organise an army abroad and launch the final struggle for India's freedom. It was necessary to look not only to the military side but also to the political and diplomatic sides. This was crucial in order to ensure that after independence, India got official recognition quickly and had the full support and sympathy of several nations.

Regarding the students in the group, Bose felt that they should be in the section dealing with political and diplomatic preparations.

Abid Hasan thought differently. 'No Sir, I beg to differ. Some of us students should be on the military side: first of all to see that our army does not become like the mercenary Indian Army. The Indian Army is nothing but a mercenary army. The officers at the high level cannot identify with the fighting army. We should mingle with the men. After all, in an army morale is something that counts. There could be political reverses, there could be military reverses, and to leave the army entirely as a secluded, segregated part won't be correct. There would be trying times and at such times, we could depend upon the students to carry the banner.'[2]

Bose agreed to his logic and it was decided that some of the students would be in the army.

By this time, Bose and the Germans had come to an understanding. About a thousand Indian soldiers fighting for the British Army, who had become prisoners of war (POWs) in Italy, were brought to Germany and stationed at a place called Annaberg near Dresden. They were to form the first section of The Indian League. The next question was of turning them into an organised fighting force. The Germans gave Bose two options of how they could assist. They were clear that there would be no third option. Bose and team had to select one.

Option 1: The Germans would supply the Indian soldiers with food, uniform, arms and equipment on loan. They would also provide technical training in areas laid out by Bose, but the responsibility of organising them into an army would remain with the Bose team.

Option 2: The entire batch of Indian volunteers would be handed over to the Germans. It would be provided with food, uniform, arms and equipment on loan. Every man regardless of his previous rank would start as a recruit. Within a couple of months, the Germans would deliver a fighting army to Subhas Bose.

Bose and team deliberated over the German offer and decided on the second option. There were no officers amongst the POWs and there was a problem of leadership. The Indian Army never promoted leadership. The soldiers were trained only to follow their officers' orders. The need and requirement here was different. They had to raise units or platoons that would be led by a Jamadar Saab or Subedar Saab who lived with them. If the leader fell, there must always be a second-in-command who would instantly take charge.

Abid Hasan gives an interesting insight into this training process in one of his interviews.

> Leaders had to be chosen from amongst us. After a couple of months of training we were to be granted our first promotions from ordinary soldiers to Lance-Naiks. This was an important step for us as our future progress in the army would depend on how well we do at this stage. The Germans who had been training us chose thirty of us for the first promotion test. The test would be divided into two parts—theoretical and practical.
>
> I was confident of getting 100% in the theoretical part, as I had an advantage. I used to translate the German instructions into Hindustani. I had the full understanding of what the instructor was saying. Repeating it in Hindustani was my revision. I was confident in the practical section too. In my spare time I would go with a gun and repeatedly practise the exercise of running at full speed, jumping, lying flat on my stomach and shooting. And many such exercises. I was confident.
>
> I was the first one called. The German officer told me: "Your section is here, your enemy is in that place, your enemy is armed with such and such weapons, you have so many men and these are your hurdles. Now go and attack."
>
> I immediately started, asking my men to get up and move. I had hardly started when the German officer shouted, "Here comes a bullet at you and you are dead."
>
> I was dead! But the section had to proceed, but could not, as I had not trained any second person to take my place … not a third. My nine men didn't know what to do next.
>
> The German officer said: "I am sorry, if you are given the charge of nine men and the nine are going to be sitting thus as soon as you are dead—you fail."
>
> All thirty of us failed.
>
> We were then given two weeks more time. In those two weeks all of us trained. I trained a second man and a third man to take my place, and the fourth and fifth till the ninth man.
>
> After fifteen days the test took place again and we all thirty passed.[3]

However, the situation changed very rapidly. Germany was having a tough time at the Russian front. It would be a long time before it became possible (*if* it became possible) for the German forces to clear the way towards India for the Indian Legion. Discussions with the Germans led Bose to think of approaching India from the east, using Japanese assistance. Thus, began the second part of Netaji's battle for India's independence.

NOTES

1. Based on Abid Hasan Safrani's diary, in custody of Ismat Mehdi.
2. From Abid Hasan Safrani's diary, in custody of Ismat Mehdi.
3. Ibid.

7 FROM GERMANY TO JAPAN

An Underwater Saga

It was a cold wintry day at the Indian League training camp near Berlin. Abid Hasan had just finished his morning exercises when he was asked to report to the Regimental Commander's Office. Instructions given were short and crisp.

'Mr. Bose wants to see you immediately at his Berlin Office. You better go just now by the first train possible. And hand over your arms to the Quartermaster.'

A little surprised at being asked to hand over his arms, Hasan did as he was told and caught the first available train to Berlin. Netaji was busy and asked him to come the following morning. Next day when they met, Netaji came straight to the point.

'Are you prepared to undertake a dangerous task?'

Hasan's prompt response was, 'Sir, I don't mind you insulting me personally, but you're insulting the whole of your Legion collectively. What do you think we are being trained for?'

'No! No!' Netaji responded. 'You've not understood me. Working in a group is quite different. What I am asking you is that if you are given an individual task involving grave risk, would you be able to manage it?'

With the slightest of hesitation Abid Hasan replied, 'Yes, Sir!'

Netaji smiled. 'Well you don't look convinced. Go home and think about it and tell me tomorrow.'

The next day when Netaji asked, 'Well, have you thought it over?' Hasan confidently replied, 'Yes, Sir!'

Netaji smiled and said, 'Well I am surprised. Yesterday, when I asked you, you were a bit hesitant.'

'I thought over the nature of work,' replied Hasan. 'You had mentioned sometime ago about going on a pilgrimage. I do not know if this is the time to go for Haj...we have lost count...but I thought you were serious. At first I was hesitant, but since you are the man guiding us, I decided to go ahead.'

Netaji laughed. 'So for me you will go? You know…there's great danger.'

'Yes, Sir!'

'All right. Have you got any civilian clothes? If not, please go and organise some.'

After a few days wait, Abid Hasan was asked to pack up and go to the railway station of Lehrer Bahnhof in Berlin with bag and baggage, and await further instructions. On reaching the station, he saw that Netaji was already there with some top brass of the Indian League and a couple of senior German officers. His bag indicated that he too was travelling. They were waiting on the platform of the train to Kiel. Suddenly, he recalled the short talk about going east by submarine as suggested by Hitler. So, it was actually happening.

On the train Netaji asked him, 'Now do you know where you are going?'

'Yes, Sir! I know where we are going. We are both going to perform Haj!' They both burst out laughing. It was the 8th of February 1943 when they set sail.

The tale of their arduous and dangerous journey from Kiel to Sumatra is best described in Abid Hasan's interview with Madan Gopal that was published in the *Mainstream* journal on 26 July 1997. The relevant extracts are being reproduced below with the kind permission of the *Mainstream Weekly*.

> *Madan Gopal*: It is said that amongst the best speeches delivered by Netaji in Germany, there was the one on January 26, and at Konigsberg, his last speech before he embarked on his journey in the U-boat to Japan. Did he hint that he would be going to East Asia?
>
> *Abid Hasan*: No. This speech was not all that stirring. It was a good speech. He was preparing the people to be on their own. There may be times when Subhas Bose may go to the front and may not be with them all the time. They should be prepared to do without him. He did not mention that he

would be going to South-East Asia. This would have been dangerous. At that time there had been trial flights from Germany to Japan. Netaji asked that he be enabled to go on one of these flights. After Germany attacked Russia, the idea of a German defeat did not cross our minds. However, he did feel that the war would be a long and protracted one. When Mohan Singh's army in South-East Asia got disorganised, the Japanese thought Subhas Chandra Bose's presence in that theater could change the shape of things to come.

Madan Gopal: Did he, when in India, think that if the war spread to the East, the East may hold better prospects for India's liberation battle?

Abid Hasan: He might indeed have. He always thought of all the possibilities and all the alternatives, thousands of possibilities. I think he thought about all these things even while in jail and possibly discussed it with others there in jail. He did not mention to anyone not concerned that he may go to the East. He told the Germans that he was keen to go, and he was prepared for the worst. But Hitler said: 'Nothing doing. Excuse me. I have many enemies. If there were a mishap, they would say that I had killed you.'

Madan Gopal: You mean this was discussed between Netaji and Hitler personally?

Abid Hasan: Yes, Netaji had influence over Ribbentrop, and could bring him around to his own viewpoint. Ribbentrop and others told Hitler that they had tried to persuade Netaji not to go, but now you advise him. And it was Hitler who told Netaji that he would not allow him to travel to Japan in a plane.

Madan Gopal: And then you went to South-East Asia in the U-Boat? Please tell me more about it.

Abid Hasan: We had romantic notions about the journey in a submarine. When we boarded it we found that the U-Boat had space enough for only one bed. It was a small room where the entire crew, the doctors and us all sat together.

We sat up all 24 hours. And we sat there motionless. There was no elbow room at all. We felt cramped. The moment we got up, we found ourselves in the way of somebody or the other. It was like solitary confinement. Even in jail the living conditions would be better. Such then was our life, and I felt concerned about Netaji's health. He had been losing weight. I asked the doctor, and he made Netaji take some exercise.

As soon as we entered the submarine, we smelt diesel all over. It looked as if the blankets supplied to us had been soaked in diesel. And when we sat down to eat, we felt that there was diesel in our food also. In fact, we were so impregnated with the smell of diesel, which we would like not to eat.

One day Netaji asked what was there to eat. It could either be beef or ham. We had to eat whatever was there. I told him the question what it was did not arise. Then I met the cook and looked into the pantry. As chance would have it, there was a bag of rice. And there was a small supply of lentils also. I made khichri for Netaji. He was happy and started offering it to the officers of the U-Boat. Although in the beginning they did not relish it, later they also liked it. I was apprehensive lest the quantity of rice should get consumed fast. Thank God, it continued till the end of the journey by the German submarine. It took us two months to travel from Germany to a point off the coast of Madagascar. This was the longest lap of our journey.

Madan Gopal: Was the journey eventful?

Abid Hasan: We had to cross the North Sea. This was the only way to get to the Atlantic Ocean. British submarines were systematically firing depth charges, and north of Scotland, we had an encounter, but we scraped through. Then, near the coast of South Africa also, we encountered a tanker and our submarine torpedoed it.

Madan Gopal: Was it the S.S. *Hermes*?

Abid Hasan: I don't remember the name. However, the tanker sank. There was an encounter with yet another tanker. This experience was very frightening. You know about the hierarchy of a submarine. In the army you give awards for the bravery of individuals. In case of a submarine, the award is given to the boat. It is a collective effort. So, if five crosses are given, the captain of the boat takes one, the torpedo man takes another, the diesel master takes the third and the person at the wheel takes the fourth. The fifth is at the discretion of the Captain. Each one is a specialist in the work. Incidentally, it was not necessary for Henry Ford to have been a good driver. One may or may not be educated, but each one specialises in one branch.

Now the engineer of our submarine had not handled the steering wheel. Once he came and mishandled it. The boat surfaced before it could fire the depth charge. The tanker fellows spotted it and turned round on the submarine. The captain of our submarine was shouting at the top of his voice 'Dive! Dive!'. And he was rebuking people for mishandling it. We all heard it. The railing of our boat touched its bottom. Netaji, who was giving me dictation, continued with his dictation. While the faces of all members of the crew were tense and panicky, here was Netaji continuing to give dictation. At one point he said: 'Hasan, I am repeating it for the third time, and you are not taking it down. You are not attentive.' I was certainly nervous.

It was a miraculous escape for us. When the event was over, we heard over the loudspeaker the captain of the ship telling the crew that they were all Germans and proud of the fact. However, they must learn a lesson from the Indian leader and his secretary who were cool and composed, so I was also included. The mishap took place four or five days before we got to the predetermined point of the coast of Madagascar.

During the three months that we were in the submarine, Netaji was revising his 'Indian Struggle'.[1] He was also drafting memoranda on various subjects. I had to type three to four hours a day. There was terrific pressure on me. The most important work was the preparation for a meeting with Tojo.[2] What would we talk to him, and how? What were the problems to be discussed with him? Netaji would think aloud. He asked me to imagine I was Tojo and then put questions to him, or he would take the role of Tojo and asked me to reply as Subhas Chandra Bose. He used to go into great details and examine all possible points that might arise. He had gone through all the possible questions one could think of, including, for instance the future of Indians in South Africa. The future of the Andamans was also discussed. We must take them. All these issues were thought of and discussed thoroughly not only in the submarine but possibly earlier also, even in Germany. If a particular question is raised, what should be the correct reply? Netaji used to dictate, and I used to type it out. He was meticulous and pointed out mistakes even of punctuations. I had to type them again, and then again. And finally, after all this had been gone through, he would tear off all the sheets. He had in the process stored all the information in his mind. The rehearsal was so thorough that I could have answered all the questions. When we reached Japan, except the manuscript of the Indian Struggle I don't think we had much ready-made material. We were not clear in our minds how the Indians in Malaya would treat us, whether they would be friendly or become hostile. We did not have a clear picture of the conditions of Indians in Malaya.

What was most remarkable about our U-Boat journey was the meeting of German and Japanese submarines off the coast of Madagascar at the date and time exact to a minute. Our periscope was sighted by the Japanese and ours sighted theirs. After some time, they came up and then our boat came up.

After we entered the Japanese submarine, there was no problem of food. The Japanese had decided to treat Netaji with great honour. When on our way to Tokyo for the first time we reached Formosa, the Japanese military unrolled the red carpet, obviously because Tojo had sent instructions that Netaji be received with great honour so as to put him in a good mood. The top military brass came to honour him and they did this in the Japanese way. Netaji was informed that the Japanese would receive him with the Japanese protocol and not the international protocol, and that this was a special honour reserved for him. We had known Yamamomo and the military attaché and did not know how the civilians and military persons would deal with us.

Netaji was invited to a banquet. I was sitting close to him. Came very senior military officers. They came with the sword hanging and they bowed as we do in 'sijda.' Netaji was about to do the same, when the Japanese Captain seated behind him indicated to him that he would bend only half an inch or so, but not bow down. This, we were told, was a unique honour to him.

The reception given to Netaji at Tokyo was overwhelming. The honour given to him was never extended to any foreigner. It was truly staggering. If you tell any scholar of Japan and of its way of life that according to Abid Hasan this is how the Japanese had honoured Netaji, he will not believe you. The Japanese never go to this extent. Netaji was a terrible person to work for, disciplined and impatient. Fifteen minutes before we left Tokyo for Singapore, he came into my room where papers lay scattered. He ticked me off and said that I would never be efficient, I will never be disciplined and orderly, and that's why he had had to pick up the papers from the floor. I was not a professional typist. Nevertheless, he fired me whenever he found a mistake. It was terrible working for him. Once he did not sleep for two days and nights and did not allow me to sleep either; he kept busy all the time. When he fired me, I decided to ignore what he said. Actually, once in Singapore I was so upset that I told him point blank that I would not work for him and also that, if I did, I would sleep when he went off to sleep, and get up only when he got up.

We could not have imagined the response Netaji got in Singapore and Malaya. His speech at Singapore was a memorable one. Netaji's speech had been rehearsed earlier in the U-boat. He used to write the Hindustani speeches in Bengali script. Netaji's speech from Germany had been translated by Habib-ur-Rehman, a Delhiite. Now that he had to address the Indian community in Malaya, he wished to use more of Urdu words and a somewhat Persianised vocabulary. He told me that once, while attending a Congress Committee meeting, he had heard Jawaharlal Nehru using the word 'chunanche' again and again. He didn't understand what this word 'chunanche' meant (but it sounded interesting). I told him that the word to be used for the common people had to be simple. My language was Hindustani. I cut off many difficult words from the speech. He did not like it and ticked me off and said that he would never get anything translated by me. Anyway, as usual he tore off the sheets. When he spoke in Singapore the impact of his speech was tremendous. Even the children could follow it.

Afterwards he always used simple Hindustani in his speeches. The enthusiastic response in Singapore was a surprise even to Netaji. Also surprising was the response of the Muslim soldiers. Agents of the British had spread the word that a Hindu leader had come, and they must not listen to him. While the Congress leaders were in jail, Mohammed Ali Jinnah had a free hand in carrying on his propaganda. Even Netaji was apprehensive about the possible response of the Muslim soldiers. However, their response was unexpectedly warm. Netaji himself was surprised.

NOTES

1. 'Subhas Chandra Bose gave his final touches to the manuscript of the second part of *The Indian Struggle* on his submarine voyage in February 1943. Abid Hasan, his sole Indian companion on the journey, narrated in a detailed interview given to Sisir Kumar Bose, Krishna Bose and me in March 1976 how Netaji instructed him to get down to work with him on his typewriter as soon as the German U-180 set off from Kiel. The submarine went through Danish waters towards the Norwegian coast and the North Sea and then went round the north of Scotland

avoiding British depth charges before moving down the Atlantic. The final manuscript was sent back to Germany by taking advantage of a refuelling rendezvous with a German U-tanker near Spain.

'Sisir Kumar Bose as editor put together the two parts of the book in the Netaji Research Bureau publication *The Indian Struggle, 1920–1942* published in 1964. The first part had been written by Subhas Chandra Bose in Vienna and Karlsbad in 1934 and published by Lawrence and Wishart in January 1935. The second part was composed in Berlin during 1942 and finished on the submarine in February 1943. *The Indian Struggle, 1920–1942* was republished as Volume 2 of Netaji's *Collected Works* in 1981.'

Sugata Bose, 'Preface', in Subhas Chandra Bose, *The Indian Struggle 1920–1942*, edited by Sisir Kumar Bose and Sugata Bose (Netaji: Collected Works, Volume II) (New Delhi: Netaji Research Bureau, 2022), ix.

2. Then Japanese Prime Minister, Hideki Tojo.

8 MEETING THE INDIAN DIASPORA OF SINGAPORE

Netaji Subhas Chandra Bose had a better-than-expected meeting with the Japanese Prime Minister, Hideki Tojo. Assured of Tojo's support, he proceeded to Singapore along with Abid Hasan Safrani. Reaching Singapore on 2 July 1943 they were greeted by Jagannath Rao K. Bhonsle, Shahnawaz Khan, Prem Kumar Sahgal and Lakshmi Swaminathan among others, who would later become famous as key leaders of the Indian National Army.

Netaji addressed many gatherings during his stay in Singapore. His speeches were very well received. Abid Hasan would translate Netaji's speeches into a sort of Hindustani that was a mixture of simple Hindi and Urdu words. In a few cases, Abid Hasan would even delete certain words and phrases, much to the annoyance of Netaji. He once cut out the phrase 'dialectical materialism'. When Netaji pointed that out, Hasan burst out, 'What can I do? Even I can't understand the meaning of the term in English. How do you expect me to translate it into Hindustani?'

The Indian residents of Singapore poured into Netaji's rallies. They responded as one to his call by donating all that they could to help win India's war for freedom. Women offered their gold jewelry and businessmen gave away large chunks of their assets. The rich and the poor alike contributed to the best of their ability.

There were many poignant moments. Once an elderly woman walked up leaning on her only son and offered all her jewels, saying: 'These are all the valuables I have. Please take them for the cause.' Netaji told her that she had the most valuable thing he needed—her son. Without a moment's hesitation, she asked her son to join the INA.

A dairy owner came forward, saying: 'These are my ten cows. I give them to you. These are my two sons and one daughter. I give them to you. This is my bank passbook that has about five to six hundred dollars in it. I give them to you. My wife and I are too old, so we stay. Take all these and go to India. You are the master of our future.'

Thus began the equipping and the training of the Indian National Army, or the Azad Hind Fauj.

In November 1943, Abid Hasan accompanied Netaji to the Greater East Asian Conference in Tokyo. Hosted by the Japanese Imperial Government, the objective of the conference was to work towards forging a Pan-Asian unity against Anglo-Saxon imperialism. Except for Subhas Bose, all the other delegates were from states occupied by Japanese 'Imperial' forces. Bose was therefore given an 'observer' status as he was technically a citizen of the British Empire. The other representative whose absence at the conference was significant was the delegate from China—a nation that had been invaded by Japan and was being ravaged at that very moment.

Abid Hasan had the opportunity of meeting many Asian leaders like Jose P. Laurel from the Philippines, Ba Maw from Burma, and Prince Withayakon from Thailand. None of them were popular leaders, but they gave Hasan an insight into these nations.

Netaji always felt that the two major powers of the area, China and Japan, fighting with each other was not good for Asian unity. He was disturbed by the Japanese invasion of China. As President of the Indian National Congress, he sent an Indian medical mission to China under Dr Dwarkanath Kotnis.

On returning from Tokyo, Netaji entrusted Abid Hasan with an especially important but dangerous mission. He was to carry a message to Generalissimo Chiang Kai-shek, appealing to him to come to some sort of understanding with the Japanese, in the name of 'Asian Solidarity' to fight the Anglo-Saxon imperialist powers.

Abid Hasan somehow managed to make his way with great difficulty to Nanking where he met the Generalissimo, who was fighting a bitter battle with the invading Japanese forces. Chiang Kai-shek refused point-blank. The mission was a failure.

Had the Japanese come to know of this secret mission, might the events that followed have been different?

9 THE INA TAKES SHAPE

Subhas Chandra Bose arrived in Singapore on 2 July 1943 with Abid Hasan and Rashbehari Bose. Two days later, in the packed Cathay Theatre, he accepted the leadership of the movement from Rashbehari Bose. On Abid Hasan's insistence, Netaji spoke to the gathering in simple Hindustani. His speech was eloquent and passionate. He said that the first thing he would do was to establish a Provisional Government of India.

> When the revolution succeeds and the British are expelled from India, the task of the provisional government will be over. It will then make room for a permanent government to be set up inside India. In accordance with the will of the Indian people.[1]

This was the last time Subhas Bose appeared in public in civilian clothes. Thereafter he was always seen in his military uniform. Bose formally assumed command of the Indian National Army on 25 August 1943. His very first public address on taking over the INA order reveals a clear vision of his goals and the challenges that lay ahead.

> In the interest of the Indian Independence Movement and the Azad Hind Fauj, I have taken over the direct command of our army from today.
>
> This for me is a matter of joy and pride. For an Indian there can be no greater honour than to be Commander of India's Army of Liberation.
>
> I regard myself as a servant of 38 crore of my countrymen. I am determined to discharge my duties in such a manner that the interest of these 38 crores may be safe and that every single Indian will have reason to put complete trust in me. It is only on the basis of undiluted nationalism and of perfect justice and impartiality that India's army of liberation can be built up.

> In the coming struggle for the emancipation of our Motherland, for the establishment of a Government of Free India based on the goodwill of 38 crores of Indians and the creation of a permanent army which will guarantee Indian independence for all times, Azad Hind Fauj has a vital role to play. To fulfill this role, we must wield ourselves into an army that will have only one goal—namely, the freedom of India. When we stand, the Azad Hind Fauj has to be like a wall of granite; when we march, the Azad Hind Fauj has to be like a steam roller.
>
> Our task is not an easy one; the war will be long and hard, but I have complete faith in our cause. Thirty-eight crores of human beings who form about one-fifth of mankind have the right to be free and they are now prepared to pay the price of freedom. There is consequently no power on earth that can deprive us of our birthright of liberty any longer.
>
> Comrades, Officers and men, with your unstinted support and unflinching loyalty, the Azad Hind Fauj will become the instrument of India's liberty. Ultimate victory will certainly be ours. I assure you.
>
> Our work has already begun. With the slogan 'Dilli Chalo' on our lips, let us continue to labour and fight till our National Flag flies over the Viceroy's house in New Delhi and the Azad Hind Fauj holds its victory parade in the ancient Red Fort of India's metropolis.[2]

He could not be clearer.

On his submarine journey, Subhas Bose had dictated notes to Abid Hasan detailing his plans to include women in the freedom struggle. He did not want women to be limited to supportive functions but to be right at the forefront of the struggle. He often gave the example of the Rani of Jhansi who had died on horseback, fighting for freedom, as a flaming example of the heroism of Indian women.

Lakshmi Swaminathan, a young medical student from a distinguished family of Madras, had been listening intently to Netaji's powerful and inspiring speech. She volunteered, and Bose put her in command to recruit and organise the women's regiment that came to be known as the 'Rani of Jhansi Regiment'.

Initially, the Japanese refused to supply ammunition for their training as they simply could not accept the fact of women being part of the fighting force, but they eventually relented. Barracks and equipment for the 'Ranis' were organised. Their first guard of honour was in saris, bearing weapons, but thereafter they switched over to battle fatigues. Netaji's charisma, and the thirst for freedom, was so strong that the strength of the Rani of Jhansi Regiment crossed a thousand in no time.

When Subhas Bose, who was by now universally known as 'Netaji', took charge of the INA, its strength was about 1,200 soldiers. It had to be increased to at least 50,000. Netaji's fiery speeches resulted in an overwhelming response to his call for men and material for the struggle. Most of the Indians residing in Burma, Malaysia and Singapore were from south India, and had always been labeled 'non-martial' by the British. Over 18,000 recruits enlisted with the INA. They were trained from scratch and transformed into a fierce fighting army. Another 40,000 Indian prisoners of war, who had been previously unconvinced of the cause, changed their minds after listening to Netaji. The INA's strength crossed the planned 50,000. Over half of the recruits were trained by the Japanese military. Promising and capable young officers from among them trained the remaining half.

Netaji wanted to fight this war on his own terms, and hence in order to avoid depending on the Japanese for everything, he wanted his own financial resources. He took a whirlwind tour of several South East Asian countries to meet the Indian diaspora there. Impressed by his speeches they donated money, gold and jewels. Abid Hasan recalls an interesting interaction with some wealthy Indian businessmen. They offered him 10 per cent of their income for the Azad Hind Fauj, in response to which Netaji replied: 'I would ask you, if I could tell my soldiers to fight and spill only 10 per cent of their blood and save the rest.' Generous amounts poured in.

The Provisional Government of Azad Hind was proclaimed on 21 October 1943 in Singapore. Netaji wrote the proclamation himself, drawing on Indian history, along with elements of Irish and American declarations of independence. He took a bunch of papers and a pencil and he started writing. As he wrote, each page was typed out by S. Appadurai Ayer to be sent to the printers. As Ayer later recalled of Bose:

> He did not lift his eyes from the paper in front of him, silently handed me the first page as soon as he finished it. I walked out of the room and sat at the typewriter. Abid Hasan and N. G. Swami went to his room in turn and brought me the proclamation manuscript, sheet after sheet, as Netaji finished it. What amazed me was that he never once wanted to see any of the earlier pages that he had written. How could he remember every word that he had written in the preceding page, how could he remember the sequence of the paragraphs? In the entire manuscript there was not one word corrected or scored out, and the punctuation was complete.[3]

It seems where the declaration ended, the 'Constitution of India' began. It read:

> The Provisional Government is entitled to and hereby claim the allegiance of every Indian. It guarantees religious liberty, as well as equal rights and equal opportunities to its citizens. It declares its firm resolve to pursue the happiness and prosperity of the whole nation equally, transcending all the differences cunningly fostered by an alien government in the past.[4]

Netaji's approach to India's battle for freedom was fundamentally different from that of Mahatma Gandhi, but both worked with unstinted passion to achieve their goal. Despite their differences, Netaji always admired and respected Gandhiji.

On 2 October 1943, Netaji had Gandhi's seventy-fifth birthday celebrated all over East Asia. Addressing a meeting at Ferrer Park in Singapore, he had said:

> Mahatma Gandhi's service to the cause of India's freedom is unique and unparalleled. No single man could have achieved more in a single lifetime under similar circumstances. Since 1920, Indian people have learnt two things from Mahatma Gandhi which are indispensable preconditions for the attainment of independence. They have first of all

> learnt national self-respect and self-confidence. As a result of this, revolutionary fervour is now blazing in their hearts. Secondly, they have now got a country-wide organisation which reaches the remotest village of India.[5]

The date of the joint offensive with the Japanese was fast approaching. Netaji's speed and zeal of work increased. He used to sit late into the night with a glass of brandy and a cup of coffee after Abid Hasan would bid him good night. Next morning Hasan would try and figure out how late Netaji had worked by counting the cigarette butts in his ashtray. The INA Headquarters was shifted from Singapore to Rangoon in January 1944. Orders came for the forces to start moving to Mandalay from 4 February 1944. The march towards Imphal and the Motherland had begun.

NOTES

1. Subodh Markandeya, *Subhas Chandra Bose: Netaji's Passage to Im[m]ortality* (Bangalore: Arnold Publishers, 1990), 196–197.
2. Ibid., 203.
3. Sugata Bose, *His Majesty's Opponent: Subhas Chandra Bose and India's Struggle against Empire* (New Delhi: Penguin Books India, 2013), 254.
4. Ibid., 255.
5. Markandeya, *Subhas Chandra Bose*, 206.

10 IMPHAL: SUCCESS, DEFEAT AND RETREAT

The Provisional Government of India under Subhas Chandra Bose had received official recognition in 1943 from Japan on 23 October, from Germany on 29 October, and from Italy on 9 November. It was part of Bose's diplomatic efforts. The Indian National Army could now be termed as a liberating army as per the Geneva Convention instead of being treated as a rebelling wing of the Royal Indian Army. The charges of treason could not apply.

The INA was trained in guerrilla warfare. Soldiers travelled light, depended on captured supplies and avoided frontal assaults. They were to go deep behind enemy lines and persuade Indians in the British Indian Army to change sides. The idea was to start a revolution in India, so that even if the Japanese lost, the British would find it difficult to recapture areas taken by the INA. Ultimately, they would be forced to leave India as the revolution grew.

To start the assault, it was decided that the Japanese possessing heavier weapons would break the outer defence of the British Army. The gap thus created would allow the INA battalions to enter and spread out for guerilla activities. INA would not be a direct fighting force.

In preparation for the assault, the INA Headquarters shifted from Singapore to Rangoon in January 1944. It was agreed that only the Indian flag would be hoisted on Indian soil. The first success came from the Arakan's Maya Valley when Major L. S. Misra's battalion defeated the 7th Division of the British Indian Army. Several soldiers deserted and joined the INA. Indian troops were fighting on both sides.

Greatly concerned, the new Supreme Allied Commander of the South East Asia Command, Lord Louis Mountbatten, pressed the 3rd Indian Division into service after replacing most of the Indian soldiers with English, Nigerian and Burmese soldiers. The 3rd Indian Division remained Indian in name only.

The INA soldiers fought fiercely and entered Manipur along with the Japanese forces. Colonel Shaukat Malik of the Bahadur Group proudly unfurled the Indian Tricolour at the town of Moirang on 14 April 1944. Soldiers saluted and sang the *Qaumi Geet.* Six groups fought the war under the leadership of Colonel Mohammed Zaman Kiani. They were:

1. The Subhas Brigade under Lt. Col. Shah Nawaz Khan
2. The Gandhi Brigade under Lt. Col. I. J. Kiani
3. The Azad Brigade under Major Gulzara Singh
4. The Nehru Brigade under Lt. Col. Aziz Ahmed Khan
5. The Bahadur Group under Lt. Col. Burhanud-Din
6. The Rani Jhansi Regiment under Captain Lakshmi Swaminathan

The Subhas Brigade reached as far as Ukhrul in Manipur but could not enter Indian territory due to a heavy defence put up by the British Indian Army.

A section of the Gandhi Brigade under Captain Munawar Khan Awan gave a tough fight to the 16th Indian Infantry Division that had fortified itself at Tiddim in Burma, about 100 kilometres from Imphal. This fortification acted as an advance defence post against the Japanese and the INA marching towards India. The Gandhi Brigade did not let them advance further, almost till the end of the war.

The Azad Brigade under Major Gulzara Singh ended up protecting the flanks of the Japanese Army in upper Burma. They suffered the maximum casualties.

The Nehru Brigade did not see action in the Imphal War. They were to follow the other brigades once they entered India and help consolidate gains.

The Bahadur Group was the only section of the INA that set foot on Indian soil and hoisted the Tricolour.

About a hundred members of the Rani Jhansi Regiment moved towards the border to Maymyo, a scenic hill town in the

Mandalay region of Burma. They were to be part of the vanguard when the INA entered the Gangetic Plains of Bengal after the expected fall of Imphal. With the failure at the front and the retreat of the INA, they coordinated the relief and care of the troops who arrived wounded and exhausted at Monywa and Maymyo outposts in Mandalay.

When the Japanese attacked Pearl Harbor in December 1941, America had entered the war. The American Air Force with their heavy B-29 Bombers joined the Royal Indian Air Force. Extensive and constant bombing by them disrupted the supply of arms, ammunition and equipment. The Japanese and the INA were forced to retreat. Besides the bombing, the monsoon became a bigger adversary. The wet and slushy grounds polluted by war waste resulted in an outbreak of malaria and dysentery. With little or no medical facilities, fatalities were high. It is said that 60 per cent deaths occurred during the withdrawal.

In August 1945, America dropped atomic bombs on Hiroshima and Nagasaki. Japan surrendered. The INA defeat was complete.

The *junoon* of the soldiers of the INA can be understood by their response during their debriefing on surrender. Major General Douglas Gracey, GOC, 20th Division asked Col. Sahgal, 'We had artillery, armour, air power and the numbers. You chaps had nothing, but instead of surrendering you kept fighting. It was sheer madness. Why did you do it?'

Col. Sahgal replied, 'Of course it was madness. A revolutionary army lives on the spirit of madness.'

Abid Hasan Safrani fought with the Gandhi Brigade during the battle for Imphal. He has described his experience of the withdrawal in *The Men from Imphal* (1971).

> We kept on marching. If the trek we took could be called a march. Those among us who suffered from dysentery and malaria had long ceased to beseech that we slow down our pace. There was no one left who could march faster than they.
>
> Such rations as we received and could carry on our back when we left Puinmana had long been exhausted. The hilly

countryside through which we plodded our way had been impoverished to the extreme by the ravage of the war. Even the rats had left the villages forsaken by their inhabitants on this route to Moulmein, trodden already by our allies. The Japanese in their thousands, on their retreat from Burma.

The Garhwalis among us and the others of the hills advised us what roots to eat and which herbs and leaves. The roots and leaves gave us diarrhoea and we blamed the Garhwalis for our woe. They resented our ingratitude and left us to fend for ourselves. We had to placate them before they again offered their nourishing advice. The diarrhoea became worse but we managed to march on, taking one weary step after the other.

An Army, it is said, marches on its stomach but we marched sustained only by a great desire and a great longing. Chased by the enemy, open to attacks from the air and menaced by the guerillas, even the medical aid we had consisted of our lone doctor with the few medicines he could carry on his back. He too suffered as we did and later developed typhoid and had to be carried by us in turns all along the way.

And while we marched there was no one among us, however low his rank and limited his understanding, who did not realise that the war was lost and the tanks following us and the aeroplanes menacing us would chase us into the waves of the Pacific Ocean.

Yet we struggled on all the while. If we so wanted, we could have surrendered. That option was open to us and it would have been an honourable surrender. No less a person than that stalwart among the firm pillars of our movement, General Logonadan had been specifically ordered to stay behind in Burma to see that those of us who had to surrender would do so in good order.

But surrender was not enjoined on us. We knew the war was lost but then there was a promise of a battle, perhaps 'the battle'. The words spoken in Rangoon. In the Special Order of the Day of the 24th of April 1945 kept ringing in our ears: 'Imphal and Burma, we have suffered a reverse in the first round in our fight for independence. But it is only the first round. I am a born optimist and shall not admit defeat under any circumstances.'

These words gave us the courage, the hope and the purpose to march on. We had the possibility of shaping our destiny and we would not miss the next round. Our response was neither light-hearted not born of hurrah-patriotism. Ours was a grim resolve. We knew the odds against us. After all we were the men from Imphal.

Imphal: It was a story written with our blood and more so with our sweat. We had marched up and down the hills there. In search of the enemy and the enemy had, as dexterously, avoided us and the fight we sought. His actions were elsewhere. On foot he was not prepared to meet us. He concentrated his efforts where his strength lay—in the air. We had of course no strength in the air of our own and the Japanese Air Force had to be deployed increasingly in the Pacific. Then, after some time, there was no challenge to the enemy in the air in our area and high above us he reigned supreme. His targets were our lines of communication. The bridges were destroyed. Roads and all that moved or crawled, even the humble bullock cart. The effects of all this we began to feel on the front. Our supplies dwindled and then ceased. It was then that we were ordered to fall back on Mandalay.

Aware of all this, the enemy started his offensive on foot. I shall relate only what happened on my sector of the front. On the third day after our rations ceased to come—and by that time rations meant to us only a handful of rice or atta—the second-in-command of the Gandhi Regiment deserted to the enemy, carrying with him detailed information of our positions and trenches. I was ordered to take his place. Although we called ourselves a regiment, in reality we were little more than the strength of a battalion, about an odd thousand men. Full of importance of my new position and my responsibility, I ordered that we occupy new positions immediately. Then the three battalion commanders, reduced in reality by the strength at their disposal to the position of company commanders, came to me for a talk.

The talk was to the point and short. 'We, and that includes you,' they said 'are without nourishment for three days. We have but little physical strength left. Should we waste it in digging new trenches? What if the enemy knows our positions? We too then have the advantage of knowing how he will approach us. God is with us and we have Netaji's blessings.' There was no further argument. My orders were rescinded.

The dawn of the next day brought the enemy. A full battalion of the Seaforth Highlanders attacked us with machine guns and stenguns supported with mortars and artillery. They wiped out our fore posts, but it was only that far that they could go. When we succeeded in sniping out their observation posts that guided their artillery and mortar, it became a fight between man and man. By the time it was dark the enemy had retreated behind the horizon of the far hills. The morning after that we were ordered to retreat to Mandalay.

It was on this retreat that we realised that the war was lost. The devastation of the road to Mandalay was complete, even the humblest ford on a stream having been destroyed beyond the possibility of any quick repair. We had to wade chest deep through the small river holding our weapons high and yet managing to grip on to the next man in order not to be swept away by the angry waters.

The countryside was completely desolate, the local population having long forsaken this war-torn area. Food of any kind, even nourishing roots and leaves, were not available. The sick were with us and the weak. We had to struggle ourselves and help others to drag on.

We were bitter. I recall an incident, one of the many of its kind, when a soldier, in this case a Garhwali, broke down in impotent tears. He had collapsed and to make him stand up and walk again, I had to empty his haversack of all the ammunition and as a final insult take away from him his gun and throw it away also. His platoon commander, a hefty Sikh, hero of many a raid on the enemy lines at the front, stood by and looked on, his face dark with rage.

Swearing in Punjabi, he demanded to know why we had left the front. 'There on the front' he shouted at me, 'this man would have died with the rifle in his hand, and not as the rat you have turned him into now.'

I stood there sullenly without replying. The front: How each man among us longed to go back to the dignity there. We had our trenches there, we had our arms and we knew our ground. There we had the enemy not at our back as now, but in front of us.

'Who ordered this retreat?' roared Arjun Singh again, his words again full of abuse. Suddenly we all became silent. Arjun Singh was speaking for all of us and we had come near to treason. 'No,' he added hoarsely, 'No, he could not have known it, not he who was so far away, while we so nearby at the front had no knowledge of the conditions.'

We took up our march again. We knew the route well, having driven and marched along it going to the front. Kalewar was not far away and at Kalewar was our transit camp. There our travail would end. When we at long last reached Kalewar, we found the camp a big shamble of dilapidated huts. And there was but little food, mainly at the sick bay. There was no alternative but to march on, especially since we were assured that nearby some kind of ferry still functioned to help us cross the mighty Chindwin, a river which we could not have by ourselves negotiated.

But not all of us left Kalewa. The sick bay there, with all its filth, stench and utter neglect, proved to be the undoing of many an otherwise tough heart. For one, I remember Cherian, an officer trained by us who had given an exemplary account of himself at the front and had, along the route, valiantly withstood all the physical ravages to which his slender body was subjected. He collapsed at Kalewa and stretched himself at the sick bay and nothing I could say would persuade him to rise. 'Mandalay?' he questioned and added, 'How far off, how far away! There is no Kalewa here, and should we ever reach it, will we find a Mandalay there?' He died the next day after we left.

It was not only Cherian, the smiling and cheerful boy brought up in the soft and easy atmosphere of Malaya that fell a victim to the terrible strain. Even hardened men, reared from their infancy in rough climate and rugged terrain, succumbed to it. There was for instance Major Akbar Ali Shah, the stalwart Pathan from the NWFP. He was the Chief Medical Officer of our Division and had taken devoted and patient care of our wounded and sick under trying circumstances with astonishing efficiency. It was more with his morale than the few medicaments available to him that he had tended us. He crossed the Chindwin with us but added to his dysentery he developed temperature. His medical colleagues who were running a forward hospital at Monewa advised him to go there with them. 'This is the end of me,' he said as we parted company. 'I shall not see you again in Mandalay or elsewhere. When you meet Netaji, tell him I really could not make it anymore, and give him my "Jai Hind".'

Crossing the Chindwin, we left off the main route of the retreat and headed directly towards the river Mu. Although the distance to Mandalay became much longer, this decision soon brought its rewards. On the other side of the Mu, we all of a sudden came back to civilisation. There was food and aplenty and the villagers were willing to sell it. We broke into small units and fell to eating hardly waiting for the food to be properly cooked.

It was then that I was called to Arjun Singh. He stood there in front of me, his tall body drooping and a vacant look in his eyes. He held out a half-filled tumbler at me with shaking hands. 'Dudh,' he kept on repeating, 'Major Sab, dudh'. He had eaten and drunk nothing and, from the first sight of milk when we arrived at the village, acted that way. With patience and the devoted care of the men of his platoon, we managed to force him to take some nourishment and put him to sleep. But he remained a sick man.

Yes, we were the men from Imphal, we who had suffered the reverses. Yet we were again on foot, this time ordered by no one and knowing well what to expect on the way—and not certain what we would find at journey's end. We had no certainty but we had hopes and the hopes were good enough for us. And where would our trail end? About that too we were not quite sure. For the present we had decided on Bangkok. To go to Bangkok we were to first reach Moulmein, and Moulmein seemed so far away. But we would reach it. Our immediate worries would be over once we crossed the tedious Karan Hills and entered the Shan estate. There food also would be available. Yes, we would reach Moulmein, we would reach Bangkok, and we would be there at the roll call.

What a group we were and ours was but a unit among many of its kind in our army. I felt proud and I feel more proud today that I belonged to it. Baluchis were there among us and Assamese, Kashmiris and Malayalis, Pathans and Sikhs and Gujaratis, proud members of classes called the martial, and those till then denied the reputation for martial valour but who proved in battle that they could by their deeds claim equal honour. Every region in India was represented and every religion and every caste, mixed inseparably together, not only in bigger formations but even in small platoons and sections, each unit being a living tribute to the unity of India. We had our different private faiths and we had our different languages, but in our purpose and in our political belief we were a well-knit, determined and indivisible whole.

What I wondered, as we trodded along strange paths in that foreign place so far away from home, what I wondered was the force that united us, we who were otherwise so different one from the other, individually and in small groups? Regions had kept us apart and our religions, our castes, our customs and our separate traditions. Yes, specially our separate traditions which our petty leaders knew well to exploit to enhance their cause and weaken ours. But did all these differences really matter? Yes, they did in the absence of any other ideology. What distinguishes us in our column, as indeed in the whole of the Azad Hind Movement, both in its civil and military wings, was that we had an ideology, a national ideology and a leader who not only imparted this ideology to us but kept a zealous guard that it remained pure in its national approach, not tinted with any other sentiment religious and regional.

No one had asked us to cease to be a Tamilian or Dogra, a Punjabi Muslim or a Bengali Brahmin, a Sikh or an Adivasi. We were all that and perhaps more fiercely so than before, but these matters became personal affairs. We ceased belonging to groups like that because India became our goal and with it our endeavour to establish India to the greatness due to her. We in separate groups did not count.

We, however, did count the moment we became part of a whole. This all-embracing India we took upon ourselves to establish. This became our purpose in life. In its turn this gave a meaning to our existence and with it we found for ourselves a new identity, perhaps for the most of us an identity for the first time. Till then we were part of the herd, now we became individuals, the interest of every one among us being to securely establish this identity. Our unity came to us as a corollary to our belief. It was born out of our enthusiasm.

What this enthusiasm was that we imbibed may well be illustrated by relating an incident. After he was interrogated by a British officer when he had to surrender, a high-ranking officer, the battle-worthy commander of a fighting regiment, was asked by his persecutor: 'And what did you obtain for all this achievement? Had you but accomplished, remaining on our side, a fourth of all this, your reward from us would have been immense.' The question did not appear cynical to our officer and without a moment of reflection, he replied simply—'But my reward was indeed immense. Netaji embraced me.'

That was in Mandalay. We of Imphal had hardly reached there, coming in our small groups when word went round that Netaji was arriving from Rangoon to meet us. We hardly believed that possible and we certainly did not want that he expose himself to unnecessary danger coming to us by road on that disastrous route—he who was our banner and shield. He who gave us our identity and unity, he who gave meaning to our struggle and to our lives.

But he came and we the sick and the weary assembled to meet him, each man turned out as smart as our circumstances would permit. The Sikhs oiled their beards, the Punjabi Muslims, the Dogras and Rajputs twirled their moustaches and we the indiscriminate put on as good a face as we could manage. As he, our *Neta*, spoke to us, our weariness seemed to depart from us and our sickness and we felt refreshing new blood circulating in our veins. So, I thought, must miracles have been worked in the past which we hear.

'I cannot meet you all individually, much as I want' said Netaji at the conclusion of his talk, 'You know I have to

> return immediately to Rangoon. It is from there that I can best serve you. But I shall meet all your officers and they in turn shall embrace you on my behalf.' So we the officers, big and small, queued up, eager for the few moments we could have alone with him.
>
> When my turn came Netaji said to me, 'Nobody tells me what all you had to undergo. I want to know. You have been long close to me. I expect you to speak.' I had to gulp a lump down my throat but managed to recover. 'I am reminded, Sir' I told him, 'of the reply our Divisional Headquarters received when just prior to our retreat our staff officer went to the Japanese Command at the front to enquire about the situation. The Japanese reply in all earnest was—"To tell you frankly, the situation is slightly not so very good." That, Sir, was the case with us also. Our circumstances were slightly not so very good.' Netaji smiled faintly and I could see a gulp in his throat. When I wanted to get up, he mentioned me to remain seated. We sat in silence for a couple of minutes. He then became composed and bade me take my leave, and the next officer went in to meet him.[1]

The INA shook the faith of the British Raj in the Indian Army's loyalty to the Crown. Later, British Prime Minister Lord Clement Attlee, while talking about the decision to grant independence to India, cited several reasons, the principal one being the erosion of loyalty to the Crown among soldiers of the Indian Army as a result of Netaji's military campaign.

NOTE

1. Abid Hasan Safrani, *The Men from Imphal* (Calcutta: Netaji Research Bureau, 1971), 1–12. Reproduced here by courtesy of the Netaji Research Bureau, Kolkata.

11 GOODBYE, NETAJI!

Netaji did not to stop his struggle for freedom, even after the defeat on the borders of India, the jungles of Burma and the Japanese surrender. He continued to plan ahead. He flew from Singapore to Saigon via Bangkok. At Bangkok he picked up his close colleagues Habibur Rahman, Preetam Singh, S. A. Aiyer, Gulzara Singh, Debnath Das and Abid Hasan Safrani.

In Saigon Netaji met Field Marshal Hisaichi Terauchi and asked him if a flight could be arranged for him to the Soviet Union. Seeing the increasing anti-British approach of the Soviets, he saw the possibility of basing himself there for his future operations against the British Raj. When Terauchi consulted his Headquarters, the request was declined. But Terauchi was sympathetic to Bose, so he proposed the idea of putting him on the plane to Tokyo via Manchuria, which was still under Japanese control. The Soviet Army was fast approaching Manchuria. Bose would disembark there and await his fate at the hands of the Soviets.

Abid Hasan Safrani's last meeting with Netaji is best described by Abid Hasan himself.

> I was in Bangkok when Japan surrendered on 15 August 1945. Netaji called me and asked me to get ready to accompany him. On his instructions, I repacked the gold jewelry and other valuable items contributed by the Indian diaspora for the war efforts. They were put into two suitcases.
>
> On the morning of 17 August, we flew to Saigon along with Habibur Rahman, Preetam Singh, S. A. Aiyer, Gulzara Singh and Debnath Das. The Japanese authorities there recommended that we all leave Saigon as soon as possible as the Allied forces were about to arrive to take over. Netaji had a couple of meetings with Field Marshal Terouchi.
>
> The Japanese authorities organised a plane for us, but no one knew where it was destined for. After some time,

> General Saburo Isoda, the head of the Japanese-INA liaison organisation came and told us that it would be too dangerous to fly a Japanese plane in the current situation as it was just two days since Japan had surrendered. There was another plane going to Tokyo transporting Japanese army officials who were carrying documents relating to the surrender. The documents were to be given to Allied representatives in Tokyo. Since the plane was carrying these documents, it could be considered safe. However, only one seat could be spared. On Netaji's insistence the Japanese organised one more seat. Netaji asked Habibur Rahman to accompany him. We managed to transport the two suitcases of jewelry and valuables into the plane. Netaji bid goodbye to his comrades by shouting 'Jai Hind!'
>
> When the doors of the plane were about to close, I shouted 'Sir!' and handed him the golden cigarette case gifted to him by Ribbentrop when he was in Germany. As the aircraft taxied to the runway, I suddenly remembered Netaji's camera that was slung over my shoulder. I cried out 'Sir!' but it was too late. It was 5.20 pm. The five of us who couldn't get a seat went back disheartened to our camp in Saigon.
>
> Soon after, the Japanese arranged for a plane to take us to Hanoi on 20 August 1945. From there we would be taken to Tokyo to join Netaji. Aiyer stayed back to catch a direct plane to Tokyo.
>
> In Hanoi I stayed with an Indian businessman who was a supporter of the INA. I gave him Netaji's camera and some gold given to me by Aiyer to help me get through difficult times. It is here that I got the news of Netaji's plane crash and death.[1]

The Mitsubishi Ki-21 heavy bomber carrying Netaji and Habibur Rahman landed at Tourane Airfield at Da Nang, central Vietnam for a night halt. While the passengers rested, the technicians detached the machine guns, heavy ammunition and anti-aircraft gun attached to the plane in order to reduce its weight.

The plane took off at sunrise to reach Taihoku Airfield at Taipei in Taiwan at noon. It was fully refuelled there as the next leg of its journey was Dairen in Manchuria, where there were no refuelling facilities. Netaji and Habibur Rahman were to disembark at Dairen. The plane took off from Taihoku Airfield around 2 p.m. and immediately after takeoff, the passengers heard a short loud blast like an engine backfire. Airport mechanics on the ground saw the portside engine fall off with the propeller. The plane swung sharply to the right and plummeting to the ground it broke into two and exploded into flames. The pilot, co-pilot and General Shidea were killed instantly. Rahman was stunned for a while. Netaji was soaked in gasoline. They ran out of the burning wreckage. The ground staff running towards the plane saw two figures staggering towards them—one was a flaming human torch. It was Netaji whose gasoline-soaked clothes had instantly caught fire. Rahman with the help of the ground staff managed to smother out the flames, but Netaji's face and head were severely burnt.

Netaji and other injured passengers were rushed to the Nonmon Military Hospital south of Taihoku. The surgeon in charge at the hospital Dr Taneyoshi Yoshimi was the first to see him. Netaji was conscious and coherent. Dr Yoshimi saw third-degree burns on many parts of his body including his chest. He knew that except for a miracle Netaji could not survive. He started the treatment of bandaging certain areas, applying ointment on others, gave him injections and blood transfusion. Despite all the efforts Netaji went into a coma and passed away shortly after 8 pm. The Japanese stood up to pay respect to his body, saluting. Habibur Rahman knelt by Netaji's bed and prayed.

Netaji was cremated at the Taihoku crematorium on 20 August 1945. His death was announced by the Japanese on 23 August 1945. His ashes were taken to Tokyo by a Japanese officer Lieutenant Tatsuo Hayashida and handed over to Mr. Rama Murti, president of the Tokyo Indian Independence League. After a memorial service on 14 September 1945, the ashes were turned over to the priest of the Renkoji Temple of Nichiren Buddhism in Tokyo. There they have remained ever since.

Post-Independence, a number of enquiries have been held regarding the air crash. All of them had their terms limited to ascertain whether Subhas Bose was dead or alive. They did not go beyond that to enquire whether the crash was an accident or sabotage.

Netaji's Last Words

Netaji was conscious while being taken to the hospital. Again, at the hospital he regained consciousness and asked for water a few times. Col. Habibur Rahman has recalled the following utterances of Netaji.[2]

While lying on the ground after the flames had been doused, Netaji asked Rahman: *'Aap ko ziada to nahin lagi?'* (Hope you have not been hurt too badly?)

When Col. Rahman said he was fine and reassured him that he would be fine as well, Netaji replied: 'No, I don't think so.'

On the way to the hospital, Netaji asked: 'Hasan…Hasan, where is Hasan?'

Col. Rahman replied: 'Hasan is not here Sir, I am Habibur Rahman.'

Netaji then said: '*Jab apney mulk wapas jayen to mulki bhaiyon ko batana ki mein akhri dum tak mulk ki azadi key liye larta raha hoon. Yeh jange-e-Azadi jari rahegi. Hindustan zaroor azad hoga, us ko koi ghulam nahein rakh sakta.*' (When you return to our country, tell my countrymen that I fought for the liberation of my country till my last breath. The fight for freedom will continue. India will definitely win freedom. No one can keep her enslaved.)

NOTES

1. This narration is based on Abid Hasan Safrani's unpublished notes and papers, in custody of Ismat Mehdi, and discussions with Krishna Bose, niece-in-law of Subhas Chandra Bose.

2. As shared by Col. Habibur Rahman in conversation with Krishna Bose, and as recounted by Krishna Bose to Abid Hasan Safrani when he visited the Bose family in Calcutta. See Krishna Bose, *Netaji: Subhas Chandra Bose's Life, Politics & Struggle*, edited and translated by Sumantra Bose (Picador India, 2022), 160.

12 INDIA WINS FREEDOM

A month before Netaji's air crash in August 1945, the Labour Party headed by Clement Atlee won a landslide victory in the British elections. The Conservative Party headed by Winston Churchill was defeated.

In India, the situation was changing radically. The wartime black-out of news had been relaxed. The media was giving accounts of Netaji Subhas Chandra Bose and the Indian National Army's bravery in fighting for independence. The British Government, despite warnings of possible public upsurge, made a last-ditch effort to instill fear by publicly announcing the court-marshal of Shah Navaz Khan, Prem Singh Sahgal and Gurbaksh Singh Dhillon. This was to be followed by the trial of Abdul Rashid, Shinghara Singh, Fateh Khan and Captain Malik Munawar Khan Awan.

Given the political importance and significance of the trials it was decided to hold them at the Red Fort. It was a sort of a message by the British that they were still in charge. The populace should not forget that the 1857 Uprising headquartered there was successfully crushed. During the mutiny the capture of Red Fort, which was the last bastion standing, denoted India's complete subjugation to Britain.

The Indian National Congress called for the release of the three accused. They established the INA Defence Committee to defend these officers. Besides defending these officers, they also took on the responsibility of coordinating information about the other INA troops held captive in India and Singapore. A defence team was formed consisting of famous lawyers. They were Bhulabhai Desai, Asaf Ali, Jawaharlal Nehru, Tej Bahadur Sapru, Kailash Nath Katju and Lt. Col. Horilal Varma. Noshirwan P. Engineer, the Attorney General of India, was the Chief Prosecutor.

Shah Navaz Khan, Prem Singh Sahgal and Gurbaksh Singh Dhillon, all three were accused of waging war against the British King, inviting Section 121 of the Indian Penal Code. Gurbaksh Singh Dhillon was additionally charged with murder. The charge of abetment to murder was added to Shah Nawaz Khan and Prem Singh Sahgal. As the trial started, photos of Subhas Chandra Bose, records of his speeches and the INA song '*Kadam Kadam Badhaye Ja*' were being sold to collect funds for the defence of the INA prisoners. Posters appeared everywhere proclaiming them as patriots and not traitors. In November 1945, people suddenly burst out on the streets of Calcutta raising slogans of '*Marshal Bose Zindabad!*' and '*Cholo Dilli Cholo!*'. The city reverberated with shouts of '*Jai Hind!*', the INA slogan proposed by Abid Hasan Safrani.

This period was the last campaign in which the flags of the Congress and the Muslim League were flown together. Despite widespread protests the trials went on, leading to the conviction of all three INA officers. They were sentenced to deportation for life to the Andaman Islands. However, the sentences were not carried out as the growing public pressure forced the Commander-in-Chief of the Army, Field Marshal Sir Claude John Eyre Auchinleck to release them. They walked out of the Red Fort with drums beating to the song '*Laal Qile se aayi aawaz, Sahgal, Dhillon, Shahnawaz*'.

During the trial a large section of the Royal Indian Navy mutinied. The mutiny spread from Karachi to Bombay to Vizag to Calcutta. What alarmed the British was the open support that the mutiny received from the public. In some places the noncommissioned officers started ignoring the orders of British superiors. There were minor but significant revolts in the garrisons in Madras and Pune. In February 1946 an army mutiny at Jabalpur was forcefully suppressed by the British troops using bayonets.

The British government abandoned the remaining trials and released all INA prisoners everywhere. Abid Hasan Safrani could now return home from his prison in Singapore.

On the ides of March 1946, Prime Minister Clement Atlee announced in the House of Commons that His Majesty's government would make the utmost endeavours to enable India to attain freedom as swiftly as possible. Winston Churchill, who had once famously remarked that 'I have not become the King's First Minister in order to preside over the liquidation of the British Empire',[1] was now sitting on the Opposition bench.

Lord Louis Mountbatten was appointed the last Viceroy of India in February 1947, with the mandate of organising the peaceful transfer of power to Indian representatives. He miscalculated and recklessly advanced the date of Partition and Independence. It resulted in one of the biggest bloodsheds in history, leaving the wide green fields of Punjab soaked red in spilt blood.

Amidst this bloodshed, Pandit Jawaharlal Nehru stood up in the Central Hall of the House of Parliament in New Delhi on the night of 14–15 August 1947 to read his speech: 'Long years ago we made a tryst with destiny, and now the time comes when we shall redeem our pledge, not wholly or in full measure, but very substantially. At the stroke of the midnight hour, when the world sleeps, India will awake to life and freedom…'

India was bloodied but free.

NOTE

1. 'From the archive: Mr. Churchill on our one aim', *The Guardian* (originally published 11 November 1942). Available at https://www.theguardian.com/theguardian/2009/nov/11/churchill-blood-sweat-tears (accessed 16 November 2022).

13 SERVING INDIA AS A DIPLOMAT

Due to the news blackout during World War II, the family had not heard from Abid Hasan throughout the war years (1939–45). They were under the impression that he was still pursuing his studies in Berlin. They had no idea that he had joined Netaji.

When the war ended, an ex-Indian Army soldier from Burma came to see Abid Hasan's family in 1946. He told them about Abid Hasan joining the INA, that he was safe, and was going to be released from Singapore jail and would be back in the country any day.

Abid Hasan arrived home in Hyderabad to warm embraces of sheer relief and joy. Everyone in the family wanted to hug him, hold him and just look at him to their heart's content. When some of the younger children tried to edge in, he playfully told them, 'I am a Sultan for a day…then all yours from tomorrow.'

After the fall of the INA, Abid Hasan was arrested and languished in Singapore jail for awhile. When Jawaharlal Nehru visited the jail to meet the INA prisoners, he found Abid Hasan coiled up in a solitary cell, all skin and bone. When he was released and returned to Hyderabad, he fell seriously ill. On recovery, he tried to work with the Congress Party in Hyderabad for sometime. But he was highly disillusioned and left.

After Independence, the Indian Government was looking for talent for its foreign services. Preference was being given to INA officers, and so Abid Hasan applied. He got through the written examinations. Prime Minister Nehru was chairing the final recruitment interviews. Referring to some articles that Abid Hasan had written that did not favour the Congress Party, Nehru asked him if he stood by the views he had then expressed. Abid Hasan boldly replied that given the same set of circumstances, he would write the same things again. His confidence and his forthrightness apart, the interview panel was also impressed by Safrani's mastery of German and Farsi.

The reasons behind Abid Hasan Safrani's selection and appointment to the Foreign Desk of a newly independent India—a challenging and crucial role—by Prime Minister Nehru may have included his boldness in defending his writings during the interview, his courage and patriotism as an intrepid soldier of the INA and his role in coining the slogan '*Jai Hind*', his education and background and, of course, Safrani's knowledge of multiple foreign languages, among other factors.

In his new role, Abid Hasan diligently went through all the notes of Nehru's speeches given on various occasions, like the Asian Relations Conference at Delhi in March 1947. While studying them in detail and preparing his own notes, he recalled the various dictations he had taken from Netaji during their long submarine journey and Netaji's views on what India's foreign policy should be after independence. Subhas Bose was no longer there. A vast horizon of possibilities had now opened up in front of Abid Hasan. He was to traverse the well-charted sea, still rough, but not as turbulent as it was during the war.

Most of Abid Hasan's postings in the Indian Embassies were as First Secretary. He was to assist the Ambassador in officially articulating and implementing India's foreign policies. It also involved attending parties of the other embassies where he met diplomats from various countries. At these gatherings, there would be informal discussions of India's policies and her stand on specific events, and though 'informal', one of course had to be 'diplomatic' and circumspect about one's utterances all the time.

Cairo, Egypt

It so happened that Abid Hasan's very first posting as First Secretary was to Egypt in 1948. India and Egypt have had age-old relations. The first paragraph of the Indian government note states:

> India and Egypt, two of the world's oldest civilisations, have enjoyed a history of close contact from ancient times. In

> modern times, Mahatma Gandhi and Saad Zaghloul shared common goals on the independence of their countries, a relationship that was to blossom into an exceptionally close friendship between Gamal Abdel Nasser and Jawaharlal Nehru, leading to a Friendship Treaty between the two countries in 1955.[1]

Egypt was a British Protectorate under King Farouk. During World War II, British troops used Egypt as its primary base for all Allied operations in the region. British troops were withdrawn to the Suez Canal area only in 1947. Nationalist anti-British feelings in Egypt continued to grow after the war.

As events unfolded, a war between Egypt and Israel was raging at the time Abid Hasan landed in Cairo in 1948. The Egyptian army was mauled, which started a train of events leading to a revolt by the Egyptian army led by Mohamed Naguib and Gamal Abdel Nasser. King Farouk was deposed in 1952 and Egypt finally became a republic in 1953.

Working in the Embassy was something new for Safrani. He would often take help from fellow diplomats in the British Embassy. Harold Kim Philby, the famous British spy who was later revealed to be a double agent for the Russians, showed Safrani how to decipher coded telegrams.

Safrani had taken his sister Ameerunissa to Cairo along with her son Shehbaz. They lived in the fashionable area of Zamalek. Ameerunissa's charm made them a hit in diplomatic circles.

The seeds of friendship sown on Egyptian soil by the Indian mission, Safrani and family blossomed, with streets in Cairo being named after Indian leaders—Mahatma Gandhi, Pandit Nehru, and Dr Zakir Hussein (as it is spelt there). Busts of Mahatma Gandhi stand at the Supreme Council of Culture and at Al Horreya Park in Cairo.

Peking, China

After a short spell in India, Safrani was posted to China in 1951 as First Secretary in the Embassy. He seemed to have a knack for landing in one hot spot from another. The Korean War was raging at the time. Following Japan's defeat, the northern part of Korea was occupied by Soviet forces while the southern part was occupied by American forces. They met at what is known as the 38th Parallel. The Soviets helped Kim Il Sung establish a communist state in North Korea. The Americans helped Syngman Rhee establish a capitalist state in South Korea. Both were authoritarian states. There were constant skirmishes on the border, encouraged by Russia and America. Finally, the North Korean forces, supported by the Chinese Supremo Mao Tse-Tung, entered South Korea on 25 June 1950. A quick United Nations (UN) meeting was called to condemn the invasion and a United Nations Command comprising forces from twenty-one countries under the command of General Douglas MacArthur was formed. The UN forces pushed the North Korean Army back to the 38th Parallel. General McArthur wanted to go further for a 'clean up' operation but was restrained as the UN mandate required pushing the forces back to the 38th Parallel only. A truce was signed on 27 July 1953, with the 38th Parallel being declared as the border recognised by the United Nations.

Nearby, another conflict was taking place. The Nationalists under Chiang Kai-Shek had been pushed to the island of Taiwan. The communist regime of mainland China wanted to invade Taiwan and integrate it with the People's Republic of China while Chiang Kai-Shek wanted to regain the mainland and sought American help. The US lost interest in supporting Chiang Kai-Shek as his forces would be no match for the mainland forces of the People's Army. Instead, the US moved its 7th Fleet so as to prevent either side from invading the other.

India played a delicate diplomatic role in recognising the Peking government and supporting its membership to the United Nations while also maintaining good relations with the Western Bloc. The intermediary role played by India during the Korean conflict showed that its foreign policy was based on the concept of non-interference. This gradually strengthened the Indian image of non-alignment—a policy that India consciously wanted to follow.

The Korean War played havoc with the Chinese economy, delaying its post-war reconstruction. Roads beyond ten miles of Peking were barely motorable and foreign diplomats were advised not to venture out too far. The letters that Safrani wrote home often talked about adventures of getting stuck trying to bypass Chinese restrictions despite their diplomatic status. Those travelling by Chinese trains were constantly interrupted by tea vendors and solicitous doctors.

Bern, Switzerland

In 1954, Safrani's next assignment was in Switzerland. He remembered some of the places he had visited in Switzerland when he was studying in Berlin. He also recalled the glowing terms in which Subhas Bose had often described his meeting with French writer and philosopher Romain Rolland in Geneva to discuss his strategy during the freedom struggle and the support that Bose received from the Nobel laureate. Safrani also recalled Netaji's visit to the city of Lausanne on the shores of Lake Geneva, where Kamala Nehru was being treated for tuberculosis and where she finally passed away in February 1936. Bose, who was in Europe at the time, was by Jawaharlal Nehru's side to condole him when his wife breathed her last.

After being at two successive hot spots, Safrani was happy to have got this posting in a quiet place. The Indian Embassy was at Bern, a city much smaller than Zurich and Geneva. India's policy of non-alignment and Switzerland's traditional policy of neutrality led to a closer understanding between the two countries. Switzerland had established diplomatic relations with India soon after Independence. A Treaty of Friendship between India and Switzerland was signed at New Delhi as early as 14 August 1948. It was an important milestone in Indo-Swiss relations.

Switzerland had established trading relations with India as far back as 1851 when their Volkart Trading Company set up its offices in Bombay. Just five years before Safrani was posted in Switzerland, a Zurich-based company signed an agreement with India in 1949 to build the Integral Coach Factory at Madras.

Reminiscing about the days in Switzerland, Safrani's niece Ismat Mehdi writes: 'This time my uncle Abid Hasan decided to take his sister Zehra along, and as I had just passed my Senior Cambridge exam, he said I could study languages at the Faculty of Translation and Interpreting, University of Geneva. I had hardly travelled outside Hyderabad, nor had I dreamt of a university education abroad. It so happened that Zehra dropped out, but my uncle stuck to his promise to me. A born teacher, he had a flair for teaching languages. 'Take the bull by the horns... master the conjugations!' he would say. The grueling drill that he enforced paid off. I was admitted to the Faculty of Translation and Interpreting.

'Another semester at the Faculty for Advanced French set me on course to savour the masterpieces of French literature. Learning languages is like climbing mountains. In my case, it was like overcoming a range of them. No sooner had I reached the peak in French, than I had to deal with the rigours of German. Again, with Abid Hasan as Herr Professor, I struggled with verbs. Intensive courses at the Goethe-Institut followed. So as not to be distracted by any influence of English in my German studies, I joined the Goethe-Institut at Murnau and at Bad Reichenhall, small towns in Bavaria. The teaching here was stricter than in France. After a stage, I rebelled and, to my great relief, my uncle arranged for me to go to Vienna.

'It was the height of winter in Vienna. Attending classes in the mornings and going to opera in the evenings—those were indeed the best of times for me to enjoy and appreciate the grandeur of German culture. But it was destined and written—*maktub*, as I learnt the word for it later—that I would have to begin again from scratch. This time, it was Arabic in Baghdad.'

Baghdad, Iraq

Abid Hasan Safrani's next posting was in Iraq in 1956. He looked forward to it as there he could organise his mother and sister's *ziarat*s to Karbala—something that they could not have thought of doing on their own.

In Switzerland, Safrani would bemoan the fact that the dispatches he sent home were hardly ever opened in Delhi, leave alone read. How could the Ministry back home take interest in the very dull unchanging news of quiet and stable Switzerland? Each month would be more of the same thing. Events like Air India expanding its route to Zurich or the death of the King of Nepal were perhaps something one could write about. But that was about it. Iraq, on the other hand, was politically exciting. Though stable on the surface, there was growing discontent among the people against the regime. Gamal Abdel Nasser had risen as a charismatic leader of West Asia. The Iraqis felt that they were lagging far behind with a king who was virtually allowing the British to rule their country and drain away their precious oil reserves.

Recalling those days in Iraq, Ismat Mehdi, who had again accompanied her uncle, writes: 'Baghdad was not the city of the Harun al-Rashid of my imagination. With its dull, sand-coloured buildings, it looked drab. Coming from Europe, Iraq was a shock. But the people were friendly, warm and welcoming, and the banks of the Tigris teemed with life and activity. The first diplomatic meet was up north, near Mosul, where the Government of Iraq had set up a weeklong stay in camps for the heads of foreign missions and their families. As our Ambassador Mr. R. S. Mani was away in New York to attend the General Assembly Session, Abid Hasan as Charge d'Áffaires was invited. He took me with him. It was spring in Iraq: the hillsides were covered with wildflowers like Persian carpets. Tents, in which we stayed, dotted the landscape. During the day we were taken on tours of the ancient cites of Nineveh and Nimrud. The nights were magical with Iraqi music and lavish banquets.

'On the way back from Mosul, we stopped to witness the leaping flames of Baba Gurgur, near the city of Kirkuk. In the local Kurdish language *baba* means father and *gur* means fire, and hence the place came to be referred to as the "Father of Fires". The leaping flames are the result of emissions of natural gas through cracks in the rocks. They have been burning since ancient times and are said to first find mention in *The Book of Daniel* that forms part of the Hebrew Bible. They are also mentioned in the writings of the Greek philosopher and biographer Lucius Mestrius Plutarchus who wrote about the adventures of Alexander the Great. Perhaps it was from these leaping flames that the concept of fire worship originated.

'Life for an Indian diplomat was not easy in Baghdad. These were the days of the Baghdad Pact and the Central Treaty Organization (CENTO). Indians were not favourably looked upon and preference was given to Pakistanis at every turn. Interviews with leaders were hard to obtain. However, the warm-hearted Iraqis could not ignore the charming Safrani household. Evening parties with Abid Hasan's mother at centre stage and managed by his sister were a great hit. Abid Hasan was able to break the ice of officialdom. While the children of other foreign diplomats were going to English-medium schools, he made me take up Arabic in earnest. Rigorous learning with private tutors, duly overseen by him, enabled me within a year to get admitted to BA First Year Arabic in the College of Arts and Science, Baghdad.

'Politics was often discussed in colleges. Arab nationalism was at its height. Gamal Abdel Nasser's charisma had gripped the youth all over the Arab world. In Iraq his speeches were banned and Radio Cairo was blocked. Iraqi students were angry and disillusioned with the monarchy, and with British and American interference. There was a high probability of a popular revolt. Whenever Abid Hasan got an opportunity to communicate with Delhi, he would give them a detailed report about the brewing unrest.'

July and August were dull months due to the intense summer heat. With the government working in slow motion, the diplomatic circles in Baghdad seemed to be emptying out. The Indian Ambassador was away in New York. King Faisal II and his Prime Minister Nuri Pasha al-Said were planning to leave for Istanbul. With nothing much happening in Baghdad, Abid Hasan decided to drive to Jordan. The Baghdad Embassy was also accredited there.

On reaching Amman, Abid Hasan had an uncanny and uneasy feeling. He called his driver and told him that he wanted to return to Baghdad right away. The driver considered it madness to drive back in the scorching sun. But Abid Hasan persisted. They were back in Baghdad in the wee hours of the morning next day.

Safrani heard a commotion outside his house and looking down from his balcony he saw tanks rolling down streets. The Iraqi Army Brigadier Abd al-Karim Qasim had declared a coup d'état. The Hashemite Monarchy was overthrown. King Faisal II and his Prime Minister were caught and shot dead before they could flee. Qasim established the Iraqi Republic. The 'Baghdad Pact' signed a couple of months ago to promote political, military and economic cooperation between the United Kingdom, Turkey, Iran, Iraq and Pakistan was annulled.

The Baghdad coup took the American government and the CIA by surprise. They suspected the hand of President Gamal Abdel Nasser in the coup. American and British oil companies packed up and left—to be replaced by the Russians.

Many in Delhi felt that the Indian government was also taken by surprise, which was not the case. As Charge d'Affaires Abid Hasan Safrani had kept Delhi constantly informed. When Opposition members of Parliament questioned Prime Minister Nehru about the Indian Ambassador's absence at this critical moment of the surprise military coup, Nehru told them about Safrani's regular and detailed dispatches from Baghdad—which were contrary to, but correct as compared with, what diplomats of Western nations felt about the situation in Baghdad. In fact, thanks to Safrani's dispatches, the Indian government was the best informed.

Many of Safrani's colleagues said that it was his finest hour; it was in truth his third. The first was the submarine journey with Subhas Bose, and the second was the Battle of Imphal.

Damascus, Syria

Safrani's next posting was as Consul General in Damascus. Fast-moving changes were taking place in West Asia. The unity of

Arabs had been a long-felt aspiration of the Arabs. Their defeat in the Arab-Israeli War of 1948 rekindled this aspiration.

In 1956, President Gamal Abdel Nasser nationalised the Suez Canal and declared that the income from the Canal would be used to finance the construction of the Aswan Dam—a project crucial for Egypt's development. Angered at this bold step, the two affected Western countries Britain and France invaded the Suez area with the help of Israel. There was an uproar at the United Nations, with the USSR threatening to intervene. The forces of the invading nations had to withdraw from the region, leaving the Suez Canal in Egyptian control. It was also a signal that less powerful countries could come together to resist the bullying of the powerful.

Handling of the Suez crisis by President Nasser evoked popular support in Syria for a union with Egypt. In February 1958, Shukri al-Quwatli, President of Syria and Gamal Abdel Naseer, President of Egypt announced the creation of the United Arab Republic (UAR) comprising their two nations.

However, the union did not last very long. Safrani found himself in a hot spot once again when, following a military coup in September 1961, Syria seceded, reestablishing itself as the Syrian Arab Republic. Instability characterised the next eighteen months, with various coups. Stability returned when on 8 March 1963 the military committee of the Syrian Regional Branch of the Arab Socialist Ba'ath Party gained control and Salah al-Din al-Bitar, a co-founder of the Arab Ba'ath Party, became the President.

The Indian mission for the United Arab Republic comprised an Embassy in Cairo with B. K. Nehru as the Ambassador and Consulate in Damascus, and Abid Hasan Safrani as the Consul General. Safrani had a good and intuitive understanding of how Arab politics could often alternate between opposing and at times seemingly contradictory approaches, something difficult for many Westerners to understand. He was thus able to send back to Delhi, much in advance, reports of political and related developments in Damascus along with their accurate interpretations.

India followed a pro-Arab policy in the Arab-Israeli conflict in order to counterbalance Pakistani influence in the region as well as to secure access to West Asian petroleum resources. A common commitment to nationalism, secularism and non-alignment strengthened relations between India and Syria. India also supported Syria's right to Golan Heights. In reciprocation, Syria recognised Kashmir as a bilateral issue. As a result of this relationship Syria also supported India's policies at various international fora.

Jawaharlal Nehru, a principal architect of the Non-Aligned Movement, visited Syria in 1957 and then again in 1960. At Damascus he was received by the Syrian leader Shukri al-Quwatli. Tens of thousands of people chanted, 'Welcome to the hero of world peace!' and 'Long live the leader of Asia!' at the airport upon Nehru's arrival.

Nehru was accompanied by his daughter Indira Gandhi. They saw a modest display of artworks collected by Abid Hasan, which included paintings done by Abid Hasan himself. What particularly caught Nehru's attention was an oil painting by Abid Hasan titled 'Two Suns', depicting two male heads placed side by side but in a contrasting way—the blue head looked like Eisenhower and the red one like Khrushchev. Nehru paused and pondered over it for a while before moving on to the next artwork. His unusually long pause caught the attention of the Syrian press.

An elegant reception was given for Nehru in the Embassy garden, which was beautifully laid out in Damascene style and had a centrally placed fountain. The friendly environment and bonhomie created by Abid Hasan encouraged the guests to circulate and mingle, which made Nehru feel at ease in this foreign land.

David Lean was shooting for his memorable and iconic film *Lawrence of Arabia* in the stunning desert of Wadi Rum in Jordan in 1960. The area was famous by the name 'Valley of the Moon'. David along with his wife Leela, a childhood friend of Abid Hasan, would often visit him during weekends. One Christmas Eve, Safrani surprised them with a beautiful Christmas tree and sang 'Silent Night! Holy Night!' in German.

Stille Nacht! Heil'ge Nacht!
Alles schläft; einsam wacht

Nur das traute hoch heilige Paar.
Holder Knab' im lockigen Haar,
Schlafe in himmlischer Ruh!
Schlafe in himmlischer Ruh!

Dakar, Senegal

In 1964, Safrani's next posting was as Ambassador at Dakar, Senegal. The Embassy oversaw relations with the Ivory Coast and Mauritania.

Senegal had gained independence from France in 1960. The Indian mission was set up in 1962. The Indian community in Senegal was very small, which gave Abid Hasan few and limited opportunities for organising social and diplomatic events and activities.

A highlight of his tenure was the signing of an agreement to supply Senegal with railway coaches built by the Integral Coach Factory (ICF) at Madras. The technical knowhow to the ICF was at the time provided by a Swiss company that Abid Hasan had liaised with during his tenure at Bern. India still supplies rail coaches and locomotives to Senegal.

Copenhagen, Denmark

Safrani's last posting was in 1966 as the Indian Ambassador to Denmark. He retired from there in 1969 and returned to Hyderabad.

NOTE

1. Abid Hasan Safrani's diary, in custody of Ismat Mehdi.

14 THE SUNSET YEARS

Whenever he spoke about his post-retirement life, Abid Hasan Safrani would talk about settling down on a farm. Initially, he had dreams of growing apples in Almora, in the hills of Kumaon. Realising that Almora would be too far north he then thought of growing oranges in Jalna in Maharashtra. But Jalna was also about 550 kilometres from his hometown Hyderabad, and hardly anyone would visit him there. So finally, he chose to settle down in Hyderabad itself.

His search for suitable farmland led Safrani to an 11-acre tract of land about five miles away from where his siblings lived. It had not been cultivated for quite some time and so it was on sale for a reasonable amount. It was a little away from the main road and next to the shrine of the Sufi saint Hussain Shah Wali. There were two wells on the land, one dating back to Qutb Shahi times with stone steps leading to lower levels. The rustic character of the place appealed to Safrani. He bought the land.

Every morning Safrani would wake up to the call of woodpeckers, kingfishers, weaver birds, parakeets and bulbuls. He started planting a variety of fruit trees including jamun, chiku, papaya and tamarind among others. He was building his paradise.

One of the first gifts he received at the farm was from the Queen Mother of Denmark. In a conversation with her in Denmark, Safrani had expressed his desire to grow roses on his retirement. She sent him a rose plant. Like most nations, India too did not permit the import of live plants. However, the rules were waived for Safrani. The plant blossomed, bearing healthy red roses. He displayed them at the prestigious Hyderabad Flower Show, where the roses were much admired.

To till the fields and cart the farm produce to the market, cattle were added to the farm. They were well looked after by a dedicated caretaker called Yaadi. Yaadi went to the extent of washing their feet with warm water and bandaging them during winters when the cattle returned to their pen after having worked all day at the farm. The way the animals looked at Yaadi showed their mute love for him.

When attempts at poultry farming failed, Safrani renovated the shed to house weavers who came from villages, renowned for their hand-woven and hand-dyed textiles.

Suraiya, the only daughter of Abid Hasan's elder brother Badrul Hasan, had married Subhas Chandra Bose's nephew. When the marriage did not work out, she returned to Hyderabad. As his brother Badrul was no longer alive, Abid Hasan asked Suraiya to join him. Having worked under Pupul Jayakar and John Bissell, Suraiya brought with her considerable expertise and experience in the field of textiles. She had also spent a good amount of time with the Handloom and Handicraft Export Corporation. Working with the weavers, giving them her ideas and designs, she produced exquisite *Ikat* and *kalamkari* cloth suited to modern tastes. Her greater success was in popularising the art of *himru* and *mushroo* weaving that used dyed silk.

On his return from his last posting in Copenhagen, Safrani had brought back a black 220 SL Mercedes-Benz. It did not go with his farm lifestyle. A humble Fiat Station Wagon was the queen that Safrani felt comfortable driving around in. The sale of imported cars was restricted by law in India. Safrani had no choice but to keep the Mercedes parked at his niece's house in Hyderabad where it was maintained in pristine condition. Occasionally he would drive it on his trips to the heart of the city. Finally, when he got permission to sell it, he found a buyer. When the buyer turned up, Safrani was busy polishing his car. While examining the Mercedes the buyer's driver said to Safrani, 'When your boss owns such a car, why doesn't he give you a proper uniform?'

Safrani was known for his wry wit. Once at his old school, when asked how India could solve the population problem, Manna, as Safrani was fondly known in the family, solemnly said that he was the last person who could talk about this since he was the fourteenth child—had his parents practised birth control, he would not be around to speak.

Safrani's pension was minuscule. Periodically he received some amounts from the Freedom Fighter's Fund. But majority of his expenses were met by selling the farm produce—flowers and fruits grown on the farm—which he would himself carry to the market. The farm was also famous for its *kala bhath*, a fragrant variety of rice loved by gourmets.

Abid Hasan Safrani passed away peacefully on 4 May 1984. The sweet smell of roses, motia and jasmine bid Manna farewell as he was taken to be laid to rest at the Daira Mir Momin in the heart of the historic city of Hyderabad—the city that he loved.

15 THE FAMILY MAN
As the Family Remembers

Niece, Ismat Mehdi

It was in a church that I first came to know that I had another uncle. World War II had just ended and my father had taken me to a local church where a thanksgiving service for the Allied victory was taking place. Just before the beginning of the service, father whispered in my ears, 'Pray for your Uncle Zainu to return. God listens to prayers of little children.'

My mother made me write a letter to him when she came to know that he was in a Singapore jail. I began the letter saying, 'I am Manni'. The letter touched Uncle Zainu. He kept it in his box of letters. He would often quote me teasingly and say, 'I am Manni'—this became my passport to life with him.

Uncle Zainu's original name was Zainul Abedin Hasan. In the INA he was known as Abid Hasan Safrani, but to the family he was Zainu Manna, or simply Manna.

I do not remember when he came back, but our routine changed. Our visits to 'Dhoop Chhaon', our grandmother's house, increased. Zainu Manna was recouping there. He taught us maths and poetry and made us sing '*Qadam, qadam badhaye ja*' every day.

The Indian government needed fresh talent to expand its diplomatic presence in the world. Manna joined the Indian Foreign Service. From his various postings around the world, he would send us colourful postcards and write descriptive letters. When I asked him if the Nile was blue, his disappointing reply said that it was muddy and brown.

When Manna was posted in Switzerland, he called me to study at the Faculty of Translation and Interpreting, University of Geneva. Fresh out of school, I joined him in Bern. Bern was a small place where I found myself in an awkward situation. Every time I stepped out and wherever I went, I seemed to attract a lot of attention. People offered me lifts and tried talking to me. The reason turned out to be my saris. Very few Indians had visited Bern at that time, so a girl dressed in a sari was a new sight for them. Manna decided that I should switch to wearing skirts. No one cast a second glance at me after that.

I was underage for applying to the University of Geneva. I also had to pass an entrance examination in French. But Manna was confident that I could qualify if I followed his method of learning languages. After two months of following his grueling drill, I was ready for the exam. The question remained of my not being of the qualifying age.

I accompanied Manna to the extension of the Air India flight from Geneva to Zurich. On board with us was the Mayor of Geneva. I was introduced to him. I told him how eager I was to join the Geneva University—the only university besides the Heidelberg University in Baden-Württemberg, Germany, to offer interpreter courses—but that my being underage was a problem.

The Mayor was sympathetic, and I was admitted as a *Hörer* (not a regular student) to the Interpreters School at the Université de Genève. The course was difficult but I got my accent right with ease. The professors said that my Sanskrit background helped me.

An exciting trip came along at the end of my first semester at Geneva. Manna had booked a Mercedes, which had to be picked up from the Benz factory in Stuttgart. We had the unique privilege of going around the factory, seeing the Daimler and Benz models of different vintage. We saw the cars that had once belonged to Joachim von Ribbentrop and Hermann Wilhelm Göring.

On our return to Bern, we got the news of the demise of King Tribhuvan of Nepal in Zurich where he had come for treatment. At his funeral service, I accompanied the Second Secretary's wife, who was a little older than me. Both of us had similar hairstyles and wore white sarees. The next day we appeared prominently in Swiss newspapers as the 'wives/widows of King Tribhuvan'!

The Indian mission in Bern was also accredited to the Vatican, requiring Manna to travel to Italy. He took me along on his drive there. In the Vatican, Manna was shown around all the sights with due decorum. At St Peter's, I was politely stopped as I was wearing jeans. Only when I rolled up my jeans and hid them under my overcoat and wore a scarf, was I allowed to see the marvels of St Peter's. Finally, the time came to meet Pope Pius XII. Unfortunately, I had to stay back in an antechamber while Manna went in for the audience.

It occurred to Manna that I would pick up German more naturally if I joined the Goethe Institut as it specialised in teaching foreigners. I joined Goethe Institut in the small towns of Marnau and then in Bad Reichenhall in Bavaria. Although I made good progress, life was extremely dull. I rebelled, forcing Manna to send me to the University of Vienna. In the midst of a semester, Manna called to say that he had been transferred to Iraq. I was devastated at the idea of having to leave Europe and abandon my dream of qualifying as an interpreter at the UN. Manna too seemed upset but couldn't do much.

Baghdad was not the city of the Harun al-Rashid of my imagination. With its dull, sand-coloured buildings, it looked drab. Coming from Europe, Iraq was a shock. But the people were friendly, warm and welcoming, and the banks of the Tigris teemed with life and activity.

After French and German, I now had to face Arabic. To begin with, Manna made me take up rigorous learning of Arabic from private tutors. Unlike the European languages Arabic was tough. First I had to consciously ward off the interference of Urdu, where similar words had completely different meanings. The pronunciation was the biggest issue. I had difficulty in taming my throat for the guttural sounds of Arabic. The '*ayn*', '*qaaf*', '*ha*' and the four different '*zeds*' were all challenging for me.

Nevertheless, after undergoing rigorous lessons I was ready to apply to the College of Arts in Baghdad for a BA in Arabic. The college agreed to interview me as a courtesy to the Indian Embassy. Only if I passed the interview would I be considered for admission. Manna set about preparing me for the interview by drawing up likely questions that I could be asked. With the help of the tutor I set about practising the answers in Arabic. But it didn't work. Manna then decided that I should practise only one answer in Arabic, which was as follows:

> I have always been interested in foreign languages and wanted to specialise in one after school. Arabic attracted me, but in India it is spoken like parrots, so I found no beauty in it. I got put off and switched to other languages being taught in India, like French and German. Destiny expectantly opened this door for me as I find myself in Baghdad under the care of my uncle. As I like poetry, I started with simple verses, then short suras of the Quran and the *Mu'allaqāt*. The richness of Arabic and its inner beauty cannot be compared with other languages. Thoroughly fascinated, I now want to go in for formal studies to get the complete picture so that I do not miss the wood for the trees. When I return to India, I will have a great future and a great opening.

Further, he told me that whenever I spoke of any form of Arabic literature, I was to quote the original text.

However, at the interview they asked me a different question, in English: 'Miss Khan, why have you chosen Arabic and why this course in particular?'

As per protocol, the question had to be answered in the same language that it was asked in. I saw the blood drain from Manna's face as he was also present there. I, on the other hand, was a record all wound up and ready to play. So I blurted out the passage that I had memorised by heart in Arabic. I cannot recall the rest of the interview, but in short, I was admitted.

Manna would keep me spellbound talking about the many archeological sites and marvels of Egypt. He told me stories of how an antique seller had hounded him for days, only to show him fake replicas in the end. It was a different story in China. After the revolution, many old aristocratic Chinese families were selling their heirlooms. During his student days in Germany, Manna had accompanied the great collector Salar Jung around Europe, hunting for rare and valuable antiques. In the process, he had learnt how to identify and pick genuine articles, and negotiate with antique dealers. I have inherited some priceless pieces from his Chinese collection.

I did not accompany Manna on his further postings. Post his retirement, he settled in Hyderabad, acquiring a farmland where he grew vegetables, flowers and fruits. To sum up his life, I am reminded of a timeless quote by the great philosopher and poet Khalil Gibran:

> You give little when you give of your possessions
> It is when you give of yourself that you truly give

Zainu Manna embodied this ideal to perfection.

His exemplary spirit of sacrifice shone through his whole life, right from the time of living in Gandhi's Sabarmati Ashram and giving up even basic things like salt, to joining Netaji in Berlin where an overnight decision led him to give up his studies and a bright and comfortable future, to putting his family above all else in his later life.

Nephew, Shehbaz Safrani

In Hyderabad there are five sites where the spirit of Abid Hasan Safrani, who I called Manna-San, resides. Astonishingly, each of these sites still stands: Abid Manzil at Troop Bazar where he was born in 1911; St. George's Grammar School where he schooled; the family home 'Dhoop Chaon' at Banjara Hills to which he returned in 1946 as an INA veteran from World War II; Safrani Bagh in Golconda where he settled after retirement and lived from 1970 until his death in 1984; and Mir-ka-Daira, a Shia cemetery beyond Charminar where he lies buried.

Unsung during his lifetime, today the name of Abid Hasan Safrani is known to many. During his tenure with Netaji he coined the slogan 'Jai Hind', which was rooted in our patriotic ethos. This slogan was soon adopted as the salutation for the Indian forces and for national days and ceremonies. It also became a popular and common greeting for patriots and nationalists of all hues. Safrani who ranked as a Major in the INA was posthumously acknowledged in 2021 by the Bose Foundation as one of Netaji's closest associates, for fighting valiantly at the Battle of Imphal, and as the author of the national slogan 'Jai Hind'. Safrani also played a vital and crucial role in helping Netaji unite across religions and faiths the Indian soldiers who served in the INA.

Were Gandhi to know who the author of 'Jai Hind' was, the Father of the Nation would surely have been proud. For in his college years, the young Abid Safrani had also served the Mahatma as an apprentice at Sabarmati Ashram, cleaned latrines of human waste, followed Gandhian principles and learned humility and altruism.

Manna-San also had a deep and abiding interest in history and culture. While being interviewed for the Indian Foreign Service, the then Foreign Minister was surprised to learn that he wished to be posted either to Egypt or to China. Ordinarily, most new diplomats preferred being sent to Western Europe or USA. Intrigued by his choice, Nehru had questioned Safrani further. 'Egypt and China are ancient cultures, with promising futures like ours, sir,' Safrani had replied. Convinced, Nehru assigned Manna-San to his first posting to Cairo in 1949, when King Farouk ruled Egypt.

In retrospect, for me, Manna-San's character can be defined in just one word: self-sacrificing. He carefully balanced his modest salary (diplomats then earned a fraction of what they do now) and for years supported many members of his extended family—a tribute to his rectitude. He educated three nieces and a nephew. I was among his protégées and wards. He cared for his widowed sister, Ameer. Other nieces and nephews were regularly sent pocket money to ease the pressure on their parents.

A lifelong bachelor, Manna-San never discussed or disclosed why he chose to remain single. Why his love for a German woman remained unrequited I will never know. However, I did meet her briefly when she stayed with us in Cairo in 1949.

Abid Safrani had ten siblings: six brothers and four sisters. Jafer, an older brother, was a sociologist who graduated from Munich University and became a Gandhian. He advised Abid to take the exam for the Indian Foreign Service because, among other reasons, he had failed in the business of selling Murphy radios.

In his dotage, his brother Jafer, also a lifelong bachelor, declined in health and required care. Manna-San welcomed him to his farm Safrani Bagh at Golconda, and supported him. He invited a niece, Suraiya, to co-manage his affairs on the farm. Suraiya had married Aurobindo Bose, a nephew of Netaji, but the two had started living separately, Bose in Calcutta and Suraiya in Delhi. Manna-San also asked his widowed sister, Ameer, to share his farmhouse.

The farmhouse was an eleven-acre property that had once been an eighteenth-century hunting lodge. At the heart of it was a massive rectangular room that had once functioned as the lodge. One approached this room through an enormous arch, appropriately called the 'elephant gate'. When the property was converted into a gated building about two decades ago, the walls of this ancient hunting lodge had to be dynamited many times before it could finally be demolished. Around this fabled room that served as living-cum-dining room Manna-San constructed two bedrooms, two bathrooms and a huge verandah facing south, where the dogs were tied during daytime.

There were two freshwater wells on the property; yet only a fraction of the land was suited for agriculture. The environs were bucolic, with wild birds everywhere, and the work demanding. Safrani loved farming. All his life he had wanted his fingers in the earth. Now he was busy planting, sowing, growing greens, vegetables and fruits—papaya, chiku and the choicest mangoes among others—and generously sharing them with friends and relatives.

A septuagenarian, he would carry by hand a large burlap sack filled with fresh flowers. Seasonal motia (jasmine) blooms, plucked early every morning, were transported by bus to a wholesale flower market ten miles away. The trip required him to change buses twice. Fatigued, on his way back he would often pause midway to call on an older sister before returning to Golconda. Exhausted by the early afternoon, after lunch he would rest, read and paint.

Manna-San, who was otherwise fond of drinks, refrained from alcohol for ten days in a year during Muharram, when Shias mourn the martyrdom of the Prophet's family. The ritual gatherings, called *majlis*, were held at the homes of family and friends. Following the elegiac recitations, the congregation relaxed, chatted and inevitably compared notes. These could be considered gossip, and Manna-San regularly attended such functions to hear the latest. Even Churchill had once confessed having succumbed to gossip, preferably after lunch, with a cigar in the afternoon!

An ardent animal lover, Manna-San maintained a pack of five or six German Shepherds whom he dearly loved and who, when released at night, guarded the farm diligently. He also loved cats, as one sees in the film *Netaji Subhas Chandra Bose: The Forgotten Hero* (2004) directed by Shyam Benegal, in which Abid Hasan Safrani is portrayed by the actor Rajit Kapur.

A huge cobra crisscrossed Safrani Bagh religiously each mid-afternoon leaving a dusty s-shaped trail in its wake. One evening, another cobra, though smaller, surprised the dogs. One of them, named Baldur, engaged in a lethal confrontation. Sadly the beloved dog died, and also the snake. When a dog died a natural death, Manna-San would bury it in a pet cemetery by his rose bushes.

Once he received a guest for a fortnight: General Shah Nawaz, a preeminent INA warrior and distinguished nationalist who worked for Prime Minister Nehru. The General presented Manna-San with a goat, one of the largest of its species, a Jamnapuri. Patrician among goats of India, she became a four-legged celebrity, a star attraction at Safrani Bagh and accustomed to royal treatment. The goat would nonchalantly leap up to her favourite bamboo chair, much to everyone's amusement, and she kept Manna-San company long after the great General returned to New Delhi.

Ishaq, a cousin, was another favourite and a regular visitor at Safrani Bagh. He would stay for as long as he wished. Handsome, intelligent, Oxford and Sorbonne-educated, he had become an ascetic who had spent many years at the Aurobindo Ashram in Pondicherry. To make him feel productive, he was given the responsibility of keeping the birds away from the falsa bushes and their delightful sweet and sour purple berries. With his flowing white beard, Ishaq would sit there all day quite peacefully, 'looking at the clouds and marveling at their formations', as he would say.

On Sundays Manna-San's close friend Dr Radha Krishna Rao, tallish, lean and a health freak, would religiously trek five miles from his home in Banjara Hills to Safrani Bagh, where an early brunch, Safrani style, was served *au frais* under the trees. Manna-San, an inveterate cook, produced roast partridge as first course, followed by warqi parathas, Hyderabadi khageena (omelette), spicy kheema (mincemeat), and seasonal dessert such as carrot halwa laced with, unmindful of the advice of Manna-San's doctors, the rich cream of the farm buffaloes. Chilled Moet champagne would be uncorked to complete the idyllic *petit dejeuner*.

Once reminiscing about the Safrani farm, Dr Rao recalled how he first started out in Hyderabad, without a professional standing and with hardly any money. He was about to be married to an affluent bride. Befriended by Manna-San, he learned that the retired ambassador had a brand new Mercedes-Benz 220 SL. Manna-San gladly lent it to him for the wedding so that Dr Rao could, in his own words, 'impress his in-laws to be'.

When Manna-San died, his Doberman pincher Laika, the most feared dog in the village, sat by his side like Anubis, one of the most iconic gods of ancient Egypt. About a thousand mourners, all villagers, circled around Safrani as his body lay on the ground upon a durrie covered with a clean white cotton sheet. My mother told me how, despite all attempts, Laika could not be moved from the spot: she seemed as if weighted in iron. The dog neither stirred nor made a sound. Unchained, seated Sphinx-like with canine dignity, she remained there—this was her way of bidding adieu to her beloved master.

Niece, Bizeth Banerjee

Manna in Syria

As the Consul General in Syria, my uncle Manna had his ears to the ground. Around 1958, I was lucky to be able to holiday in Damascus and spend more than a month with him and my cousin Maliha, who was staying with him at the time.

While other diplomats partied and socialised amongst themselves, and Manna indeed joined them from time to time as he was obliged to, unlike them he also quietly developed local contacts amongst different strata of Syrian society. It was important for him that his dispatches carried correct information of strategic importance to India. He seemed to be able to develop just the right contacts to help him with the specific information sought or which the government needed to know. One of his favourite spots for a 'friendly visit' on weekends was a farm on the outskirts of Syria, to talk to an influential farmer who was politically very aware and had valuable information and insights to part with. The conversation would start very cordially, but soon the farmer would get all worked up about 'Zionist expansionism' and the designs and moves of 'the enemy'. On the long drive back home, Manna would be pensive, mulling over what he had heard and weighing it out carefully in his mind.

His other niece, my cousin Maliha, who was then studying Arabic under his tutelage, was having a tough time with the language, but Manna would not relent in his strict regimen one bit. David Lean, the legendary Hollywood director and husband of one of Manna's boyhood crushes, Leila, happened to be staying with him for a few days while shooting *Lawrence of Arabia*. When Lean did not see my sister at dinner one evening, he asked my uncle if she had perhaps gone out. 'No,' he said, 'She is having one of her crying fits'. Softhearted Lean could not stomach continuing with his dinner while someone else was crying for whatever reason. 'Please call her…we can't possibly continue unless she joins us,' he said, putting down his fork. Manna told him that it was a habitual trait, and that she would start crying at the drop of a hat. Lean was thoughtful for a moment, then exclaimed, 'Oh! I think I know how to cure that. Get me a glass of something sugary and call her over. Let me try this'. A glass of sweetened orange juice was brought soon enough, and my sister summoned. Maliha sat silently at one corner of the table, tears flowing from her beautiful eyes but without any of the redness or puffiness associated with it, which has often been remarked upon. 'Please drink this,' said Lean, gently pushing the glass towards her. Maliha quietly did as told—and within minutes she was back to her smiling self! My uncle, who used to recount this story often, said he was completely taken by surprise at this sudden transformation since he had become quite used to her tearful protests 'stretching for hours' whenever the learning got tough. So it turned out that Lean had had the same problem with his secretary, until the doctor told him that the frequent crying fits could be a result of a sudden dip in sugar! For years thereafter, Manna would marvel at the simple solution and women's 'strange constitutional needs'.

Prime Minister Jawaharlal Nehru decided to build closer ties with the Arab world and came on a state visit to Syria. As a keen historian, he was determined to find time to visit famous historical sites starting with Baalbek. Manna, as the Council General, had to accompany the group, which was being guided by the Cultural Attaché and a reputed local guide. Manna was not far behind them and so when Nehru shot off a few questions to which he did not receive satisfactory answers, he began to get impatient and angry. A naturally modest Manna, with his enormous interest in history and esoteric knowledge of local customs, quickly stepped in and started answering the volleys coming from Nehru. After that, Nehru always made sure that Manna was there to guide him. 'Is Abid accompanying us?' he would demand.

People who had come to know him well would at some point or another invariably ask him why he had not married. Uncle Manna would reply honestly that he had to take care of his rather large family and that he couldn't have done so had he married. Even as a young diplomat on a very tight budget, he would send pocket money to all the young ones growing up. About seven years old then, I remember telling him on one of his visits home that the pocket money never came on time and that it would come in lump sums. So we couldn't plan to buy what we wanted. It would be so much better for me and the others if he could just send the pocket money every month instead. Manna didn't say a word. But the practice of not getting pocket money every month, as requested, but always in bulk when least expected, to which we so eagerly looked forward, continued for years. I asked him years later why he didn't send it regularly despite some of us requesting him time and again. Manna replied that he was a firm believer in what his brother, a sociology professor, had termed 'the Law of Mounting Ingratitude', which was a reframing of the classical law of economics: the Law of Diminishing Returns! He said it could be proven empirically that: 'I give you Rs 100 for 12 months, the joy gives way to expectation, and then to resentment if I suddenly decide to withhold it! Think about it.'

Political unrest and conflicts were raging within and outside Syria at the time but due to his efficient information gathering network, Manna always seemed to know when any major outbreak was to be expected. Every time there was a coup, he was present not in Damascus but would be found in nearby Beirut. When challenged about not being at the place of action, he would say: 'I will be more effective in Beirut and communicate with the government better than in Damascus where extensive curfew make flights inoperative and the radio and TV stations are the first to be occupied in any coup.'

Manna had no patience with his younger relatives who did not apply themselves with full energy. He had taken a young nephew under his care, but soon grew concerned about the lad's lack of focus and application. Relations between the two hit a rough patch. Then one day the nephew made a dramatic announcement that he was going to commit suicide because he was unable to cope anymore. Manna was quiet for a few days. But when the nephew again repeated his intention, he told him that if he was serious Manna would himself drive him to the top of a nearby mountain range from where he could jump off. 'Of course I am serious!' replied the hothead. Manna quietly announced that he should then prepare himself for the event the coming Sunday.

Having seen the rough and tumble of life in his years with the INA, Manna could not tolerate what he thought was spoilt or self-indulgent behaviour in the extreme. Come Sunday, he summoned the young man and drove him all the way to the top of a cliff. Looking at his watch, he said, 'I will give you half an hour. After that either you jump off or come back to the car a saner man.'

Half an hour later the dejected youth quietly came back to the car. However, that was not the end of the story. Manna had to repeat this a couple of times before the fellow came to his senses. Manna had no tolerance for the weak-kneed.

Manna in Dakar

By the time Manna became Ambassador to Senegal, and accredited to adjoining countries like Mauritania, Upper Volta and the Ivory Coast, he had become quite seasoned in diplomatic affairs. He preferred one-on-one dealings and his knack of striking a rapport with the most unlikely people helped him a lot in gauging and grasping the undercurrents and urgings of the Black movement of the newly independent African nations keen to rediscover their identity. President Senghor was at the forefront of the movement to rediscover a common cultural heritage. The capital Dakar played a leading role in getting African nations together and the excitement was palpable.

The world too was watching, interested and also concerned about the shape of things to come. Manna made determined and successful attempts at developing local contacts, ably helped by his colourful and feisty sister who was his official hostess and played her own part in developing relations with fellow diplomats, their wives and the local officials. Dakar had become one of the centres of Negritude, and there was excitement and hope all around. The first festival of Negro Arts was hosted by Dakar, which was suddenly engulfed by culturati from a host of African and European countries. The festival showcased the rich dance and musical heritage of the people as well as their sculpture and art. Each day would bring in a new yacht or ship bearing participants and guests and observers and there were cocktails and dinners every evening.

The Russian Ambassador's wife, who felt comfortable with Manna, as indeed most people did, complained bitterly to him of how she was expected to attend all the functions in just one long dress, which was all she had, given the meagre budget allowed by the then very red Russian government. The dress code for most functions was black tie for men and long dresses for women. She added that she envied Manna's sister, who could turn up in any one of her large collection of saris...but what was she to do? For once, Manna had no answer!

This is not to say that in those years, the late 1960s, the Government of India was much better in its allowances to diplomats. When a business delegation arrived in Dakar to negotiate trade deals with the Indian government and to explore common trade areas, one of the gentlemen requested Manna to part with some of his foreign exchange allowance and savings, which he would make good in Indian currency (naturally at a profit!). Manna politely and firmly refused. The businessman was completely taken aback at what he thought was the rejection of an' excellent deal'. 'God knows who made such a fool an Ambassador!' he shouted, unable to understand the Indian diplomat's uncompromising honesty.

Manna's sympathetic ear had at times to listen to not only officials cribbing about some colleague or minister, but also to the wives of other diplomats who would come to him with their grievances. He would listen to them patiently and proffer advice and counsel.

Around this time some officers of the Russian army came to Senegal, probably to train the armed forces of the fledgling state. A number of young officers accompanied the senior staff and the Russian Embassy decided to introduce them to the Senegalese officers and other diplomats. Since it was to be a large affair, I tagged along with my uncle. We had to go past officers lined up to receive us. The sight of the younger ones, possibly Asiatic Russians, with their honey-coloured skin, green-blue eyes and dark hair severely swept back, dazzling in their uniforms decorated with medals, took my breath away. A couple of my friends who were also present were equally enchanted. 'I have just spoken to my mother,' said my young Italian friend, and she has decided to host them for a dance dinner evening. Now your uncle is a good friend of the Russians...Please, please persuade them to let the officers join us for an evening.' On returning home, I passed on the message to my uncle. 'Why not,' he said, 'But you must request the Ambassador's wife yourself. I am not going to do that'. I decided after a great deal of thought to just come straight to the point with her. Her answer stunned me: 'My dear, we make sure in Russia that our officers are happily married before they leave our soil…otherwise, who knows, they might fall for the charms of young women like you!'

With a crestfallen face, I repeated what I had heard to uncle. Manna said, 'Now do you get an idea of what the Iron Curtain is like? They don't know which deluded capitalists they will meet and get infected with. I did not for a moment think that you would succeed.'

'Why didn't you tell me in the first place?' I demanded. 'Learning first-hand is always better.' He philosophically said, 'Who knows…she might send you some caviar or their over-powering perfumes to make you feel better'. He was not far wrong, for soon enough I received a crate full of Russian books!

The German Ambassador was a frequent visitor, always angling for information on Kashmir, and Manna had to patiently explain to him time and again why the idea of a plebiscite was not workable given the changed circumstances due to Pakistan's incursions and propaganda. The Ambassador also could not fully appreciate the problems of a recently independent subcontinent, struggling to alleviate years of deprivation and exploitation. 'India is a bottomless pit, Mr. Ambassador!' he would burst out, 'The more aid we give, the more she wants!' This would be followed by a long and patient explanation by Manna, and one wondered how much of the visitor's prejudiced mind had been dented with fresh information.

As head of the mission, Manna made it his business to monitor the welfare of the staff and their needs. He soon found out that among the very few Indian students in Dakar, there was a bright young Malayali girl who had been consistently winning gold medals in her school. She was all of fifteen, with a couple of years to go before joining university. Proud of her achievements, Manna invited her along with her father to cocktails and he made sure she was introduced to the Rector of the University. Among all the grownups in the diplomatic cocktail circuit, the schoolgirl with her pigtails stood out as an unusual sight! The Rector politely agreed to talk to her and, on doing so, he became so interested that they retired to a corner and engaged in animated conversation, much to the curiosity of others present. At the end of the long exchange, the Rector told Manna, 'As soon as she finishes school, make sure that she sees me before anything else. I will ensure that she gets all the assistance she deserves from us. She is exceptional!' Passionate about the education of the young, Manna beamed with ill-concealed pleasure and satisfaction—this incident had made his month. It would also give the young girl a boost in her career.

I was also present at a '*soiree dansante*', to which I had been invited as the niece of Abid Hasan Safrani. The American Ambassador, bored with the thought of having to dance first with the buxom Russian Ambassador's wife and then the others in strict protocol, decided to be a little reckless and invited me, 'a fresh face', to dance with him. At this, the American Ambassador's wife dissolved into tears and came to complain to Manna. He took her aside, held her hand and God knows how he consoled her, but she looked decidedly brighter at the end of it!

Manna's sister soon became a favourite among the Senegalese and their families. Such was the atmosphere of warm, friendly informality in their house—an enormous relief to almost everyone, fed up with the constant mask of diplomatic nicety they had to wear—that one day a Nigerian Minister was seen running around the dinner table, chased by my aunt after some playful banter! People simply loved being invited, and it was not only because of the fine table that they kept.

Mauritania, to the south of the Sahara desert, was one of the countries that our embassy was accredited to. Manna would visit the country from time to time but when he received an invitation to the annual Presidential Ball, he decided to take me along. I was agog with excitement. He told me that I would have to prepare to answer in French and at least memorise some stock answers for the sake of polite conversation.

Fellow diplomats were dismissive of Mauritania. 'They are exporting peanuts,' I heard a diplomat saying. 'Eighty per cent of their exports are peanuts.' Manna did not agree that Mauritania could be dismissed so easily. 'It has vast mineral reserves. They will definitely start exploiting that soon. Their desert is full of underground treasures.'

The journey to Mauritania was unlike anything I had seen before. Vast stretches of desert iridescent in the moonlight. Manna's interest in and deep knowledge of local history made him fascinating to listen to and he would point out clusters of Bedouins or some ruins and talk about their history or speculate on their origin. In between would be my French lessons, which in this case were limited to learning up the stock answers for the ball. But I was a pretty hopeless case!

Nouakchott, the capital of Mauritania turned out to be a small little town that one could virtually walk around within an hour. Manna took me to the marketplace where there were a lot of French women running the stalls, but they all looked decidedly frumpy compared to the elegant, long-necked regal Mauritanian women of African and Arab descent, with their mixed blood, holding their flowing boubous like queens. When I told him how unkempt the French shopkeepers looked, he calmly replied, 'Observe them closely…you will not be able to recognise them in the evening'. Astonished, I asked, 'You mean *they* will be invited to the President's Ball?' I could not fathom this and to my mind the evening had already lost some of its sheen. But I remained openmouthed and wonderstruck.

Come evening, we were ushered into what looked like a scene straight out of *Arabian Nights*. White tents and lavish décor. My uncle, totally unimpressed with the pomp on show, said, 'Imagine, in a poor country like this, all this vulgar unnecessary wastage. They have flown in food from France…what stupid extravagance'. But I remained openmouthed and wonderstruck and, just as Manna had said, I saw a lot of French women and had to look really hard to make out that a number of them had transformed themselves completely for the event. When it was time to queue up and be introduced to the President and his French wife, I could only mutter, '*Merci beaucoup pour m'inviter ce soir*'. The President stood for a moment longer, expecting something more than that…but nothing came! Uncle was terribly disappointed and a stony silence lasted the long way back to Dakar the following morning.

Manna had developed his own language teaching methods, which he had further honed while teaching German, French and Arabic to two other relatives before me. But I was a hard nut to crack those days and had no stomach for the conjugations that he wanted me to master as the first step to learning French. I revolted soon enough. 'It's a crazy language,' I said, 'I love, you love, he loved, he loved recently, he loved once, he loved a long time back, he will love God knows when…why can't there be just one past and one future instead?! What is so "perfect" about the past (*parfait*) and so "imperfect" (*imparfait*) about it?'

'Don't exaggerate, stop being silly and sit down!' he told me firmly. 'It is a very logical language like Sanskrit. And English is less logical…and there are the perfect pasts and futures in English as well.' Manna then told me about his days in prison and how his jail inmates started teaching him Sanskrit since he was keen to use his time productively. 'I will recite my favourite Sanskrit shloka to you,' he said and started off with,

OM Sahana Vàvatu
Sahanau Bhunaktu
Saha Viryam Karavavahai
Tejasvi Navaditamastu
Ma Vidvishavahai
OM Shanti Shanti Shantihi

He then went on to explain the meaning and said that it was a prayer for learning and seeking knowledge together, for seeking divine protection and energy, and seeking that there be no animosity. 'Don't you think it is a beautiful thought?' I did indeed and in fact went on to opt for Sanskrit as my second language in college.

One evening, at a crowded dinner to which the French Ambassador had also been invited, Manna received an unusual request. The French Ambassador had a booming voice which could be heard a block away and which drowned all others near him. 'Your Excellency, does my nephew, who is to be with me for a year, have your permission to date your niece? As you know, there are few young people here.' Obviously, he did not know that Indians are generally very conservative in these matters, but my uncle was decidedly was not one of them. 'If she has no objection,' said Manna, bewildered by the request. 'That's settled then. He will call on her tomorrow,' said the French Ambassador.

The 'dating' however lasted all of two outings. Neither of us felt inclined to continue.

The glamour and dazzle of the diplomatic world then (gentler times compared to the present) did not dent Manna's practical, down-to-earth approach and his exceptional sense of political reality behind all the glitter. The world around him was changing fast. The increasing corruption and chicanery in the government and administration back home was not, as he would tell his close friends, what the INA had fought for. But nevertheless, Manna remained hardnosed and completely committed to his duty right till the end of his diplomatic career, which ended with his posting to Denmark.

Back in India

Practical to the core, Manna had been planning for his retirement years before he had to hang up his office shoes. The years that he spent talking to farmers in Syria and earlier when he learnt their farming techniques while gathering information about local affairs and politics would now come in handy. He started with traditional crops on a modest-sized plot, which soon became a centre for the family to gather on weekends, or for those wanting to study, or just to 'hang out'.

Just as he enjoyed hosting and feasting, Manna was also fond of cooking, and from time to time he could be seen preparing his favourite dishes. He often cooked Chinese soups and dishes. He once narrated an incident when as a very young diplomat posted in China he had seen Vijaylaxmi Pandit, who was visiting at the time and had invited fifty guests for dinner, completely distraught when all the staff hired for cooking and serving walked out on her.

Not used to cooking, she had to take all her guests to an expensive restaurant and recounted the incident bitterly. Manna said that it had taught him to be self-sufficient and he decided that he would have to learn, among other things, the culinary arts if he had to survive in China.

Frail though he was in his last years, he would never shy away even from arduous farm tasks. In the early evenings he would teach mathematics and other subjects to his young relatives who needed help. When his grandnephew came visiting from the United Kingdom with his very 'propah' English wife, Manna volunteered to show her around the town and take her shopping since she was feeling left out and neglected. Manna, she told us, would sit patiently waiting for her like an obedient chauffeur while she took hours over shopping. She had asked him many times to let her take a taxi home, but he refused, saying she was a guest. Overcome by his extraordinary warmth and affection, she burst into tears one day and told all of us, 'I can't take this anymore! I am not used to people going out of their way to this extent. I will never be able to do even a fraction of all this in England for any of you'. 'We don't expect you to either…' said my uncle stoically. 'England is England and India is India. Here our rules are different.' But she continued to agonise over the issue for many days. She simply could not understand how anyone, leave alone a retired Ambassador, could endure such personal discomfort to give her so much time and attention, without expecting anything in return.

16 IN THE WAR ROOM WITH THE FUHRER*

The Fuhrer's headquarters were near the fighting line at a military base, in Rastenburg in Prussia. This was a handicap for Netaji as his initial interaction had to be with officers and generals at the German army headquarters in Berlin.

The meeting with the Fuhrer took place on 29 May 1942 in his study. Two maps hung on the wall. One was of Europe and Asia, and the other was a detailed map of Germany's war fronts.

As the meeting progressed, Netaji's to-the-point way of talking appealed to Hitler. He was also impressed by the fact that Netaji was clear that he did not want any direct support from the German army. He only wanted their assistance in training the INA, German arms and equipment.

Those present at the meeting were Joachim von Ribbentrop, Reich Minister of Foreign Affairs, and Herr Schmidt, an expert interpreter and close aide of Hitler. Netaji's German was good enough for light conversation. Hitler did not speak English at all. Netaji felt that for the matters that he wanted to discuss, it was essential to make sure that every word he spoke was correctly conveyed. To mitigate any risk of misunderstanding due to the usage of incorrect words, he preferred to speak through an interpreter. Herr Schmidt was most suitable for that task and did a perfect job.

The purpose of the meeting was for the two leaders to meet and talk about German recognition and support for the Free India Movement in principle. Hitler, however, went ahead to have an in-depth discussion on every point and detail for the benefit of

*Based on Abid Hasan Safrani's unpublished private notes and papers, in custody of Ismat Mehdi.

Netaji. For instance, in the preliminary talks with the German generals, it was proposed that initially Netaji be allowed to form a legion of only 500 men. Hitler ruled that out. He was of the view that either they were going to help completely or not at all. This favoured Netaji.

Then the question came about marching to India. Hitler said that once he had defeated Russia, the way to India would be open. However, this would take some time. A quicker option was to go through Japanese-occupied territories. If Japan was victorious in East Asia, then marching into India would be a cakewalk. But for this plan to work, Netaji needed to be present in East Asia, and flying east was full of danger as there were many Allied-held areas on the way. A better way would be to go by German and Japanese submarines. A trip had already been planned to get a Japanese team to Germany for exchange of technical knowhow. Hitler picked up a cane and traced a route on the map via the Cape of Good Hope. It would take between seven to eight weeks for the underwater journey.

The meeting originally slotted for half an hour extended to over two hours.

IMAGE 1: 'Abid Manzil' in Hyderabad, where Abid Hasan Safrani was born. Photograph courtesy, Dr Wilfred de Souza.

IMAGE 2: Fakhrul Hajia Begum, or Ammajan, mother of Abid Hasan Safrani

IMAGE 3: Ammajan, with sons Abid Hasan (to her right), and Badrul Hasan, who preceded Abid Hasan at Sabarmati Ashram

IMAGE 4: Abid Hasan Safrani in the garden at 'Abid Manzil', Hyderabad

IMAGE 5: Abid Hasan Safrani, before leaving for Germany

IMAGE 6: Netaji Subhas Chandra Bose in Magdeburg, Germany

IMAGE 7: Netaji meeting Indian soldiers of the Azad Hind Fauj under training in Berlin

IMAGE 8: Prisoners of war recruited from the German war camp at Annaburg, Germany

IMAGE 9: The Azad Hind Fauj in Magdeburg, Germany

IMAGE 10: Lilian Frydan with Abid Hasan Safrani

IMAGE 11: Abid Hasan Safrani with Netaji, on the deck of the submarine in which they travelled from Germany to Singapore in 1943

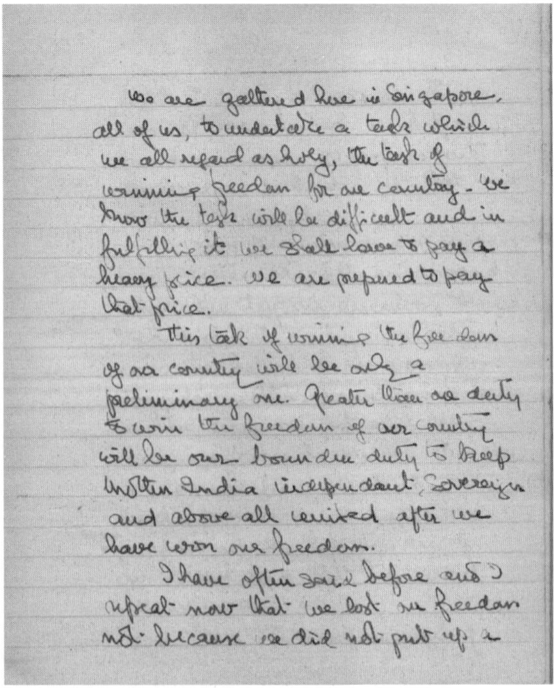

We are gathered here in Singapore, all of us, to undertake a task which we all regard as holy, the task of winning freedom for our country. We know the task will be difficult and in fulfilling it we shall have to pay a heavy price. We are prepared to pay that price.

This task of winning the freedom of our country will be only a preliminary one. Greater than our duty to win the freedom of our country will be our bounden duty to keep Mother India independent, sovereign and above all united after we have won our freedom.

I have often said before and I repeat now that we lost our freedom not because we did not put up a

IMAGE 12: The opening of Netaji's 1943 speech in Singapore, 'The Task after Winning Freedom', recorded in Abid Hasan Safrani's handwriting

IMAGE 13: Soldiers (formerly, prisoners of war) in front of the Free India Centre

IMAGE 14: Captain Lakshmi Sahgal, Azad Hind Fauj

IMAGE 15: Young recruits of the Azad Hind Fauj getting ready for training

IMAGE 16: Netaji enjoying a brief moment of quiet

IMAGE 17: Abid Hasan Safrani as First Secretary, with Second Secretary Ram Pratap, at the Swiss Foreign Office in Bern, 1959

IMAGE 18: Ammajan, on pilgrimage in Karbala, Iraq, 1956

IMAGE 19: Abid Hasan Safrani, with his sister Ameerunissa Begum and niece Ismat Mehdi in Baghdad, 1958

IMAGE 20: Abid Hasan Safrani receiving a Chinese diplomat in Damascus

IMAGE 21: Abid Hasan Safrani with the submarine captain, for a Channel 4 interview in London, June 1964

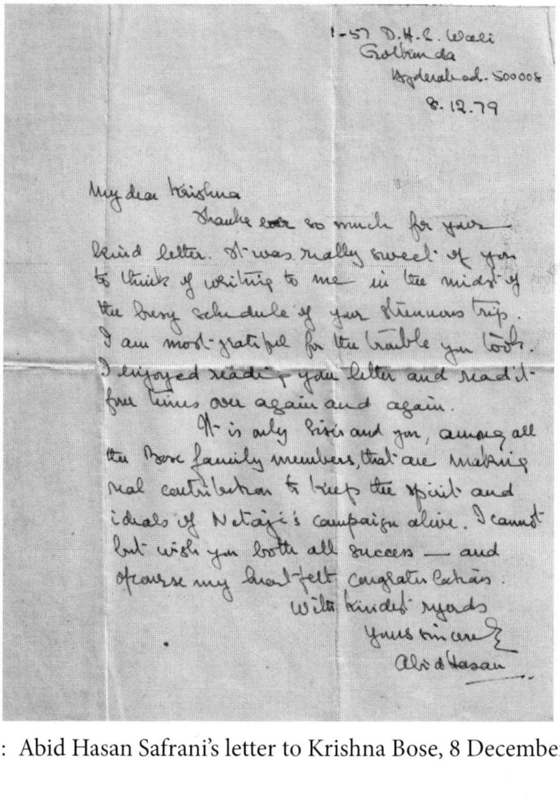

1-57 D.H.S. Wali
Golkonda
Hyderabad-500008
8.12.79

My dear Krishna

Thanks ever so much for your kind letter. It was really sweet of you to think of writing to me in the midst of the busy schedule of your strenuous trip. I am most grateful for the trouble you took. I enjoyed reading your letter and read it five times over again and again.

It is only Sisir and you, among all the Bose family members, that are making real contribution to keep the spirit and ideals of Netaji's campaign alive. I cannot but wish you both all success — and ofcourse my heart-felt congratulations.

With kindest regards
Yours sincerely
Abid Hasan

IMAGE 22: Abid Hasan Safrani's letter to Krishna Bose, 8 December 1979

IMAGE 23: Abid Hasan Safrani and G. S. Dhillon at the Netaji Research Bureau, Calcutta

IMAGE 24: Sisir Kumar Bose and Krishna Bose, standing next to Subhas Chandra Bose's footsteps displayed at the Netaji Research Bureau in Calcutta, 1997

IMAGE 25: The Netaji Award 2021, received by Major Abid Hasan Safrani

17 LILIAN FRYDAN*

Abid Hasan was training at a German military camp away from Berlin when he received a letter from his lady love in Berlin. When his colleagues came to know they teased him, asking him to reply to her soon. He was still wondering what to write when he received urgent instructions to pack up and leave at once for Berlin. Netaji wanted him there immediately for an important assignment. He was not told what the assignment was as it was confidential.

Before the train journey to Berlin, Abid Hasan shaved off his beard and groomed himself. What follows is his own account, as taken from Safrani's unpublished private notes and papers.†

> My immediate problem as I made my way to the barracks to collect my things was how to explain to Lilian Frydan my sudden arrival in Berlin. Three weeks had passed, and I had not replied to her letter. She took these things seriously. I thought of drafting a nice long letter in the train.
>
> In the train I set to work on the letter. It turned out the way she liked it to be—serious, chatty, long, devoid of sentimentality and…incomplete. I hoped that even with her sharp wit she would not be able to suspect that it was rigged up at the last moment.
>
> From the Berlin station I drove straight to the theatre. At the ticket office I met a Major who had come to return two first row balcony seats for the opera that evening. I bought the tickets and went to the Centre. I was told to report to Netaji directly. To my luck, he was away, and it was not certain if he would return that evening. I left word that I

---

*Name changed to respect the concerned individual's privacy.

†In custody of Ismat Mehdi.

could be found at the State Opera if wanted, and I went to my room that I had retained.

I contacted Lilian at her bureau before she left for home. She said she was free that evening but tired. We could meet the next evening. I told her that I had got two tickets for the State Opera that night. She need not sit through the whole programme. If she felt tired, we could get away after the first or second act.

'State Opera!' she said sounding excited, 'You soldiers do have privileges. Well, I am a selfish person. I shall come.' She agreed that instead of my going over to her place, she would be willing to come to my place for tea before we went to the opera.

I arranged the table with a nice tablecloth and serviettes, plenty of flowers and my landlady's best crockery and cutlery. The food was only bread, three tins of fish and some fruit. It was a luxury in those days.

All the arrangements did have a good effect on Lilian as she relaxed and made herself comfortable. I did not keep the tea ready as I wanted an opportunity to leave the room after she arrived. As planned, I went to make tea, telling her that in her plate was a letter that I had started writing to her sometime back but could not complete. The smile she threw me was a rather disdainful one.

When I returned with the tea, I found Lilian her old self. She was annoyed at my not sending the letter even if it was incomplete. A kind of 'annoyance' that any man would relish.

After the opera, we went to a leading hotel. The steward, while leading us to a table, looked searchingly at the Azad Hind emblem on my uniform. 'All right,' I told him, 'You may alert the military intelligence. But to make sure that I don't run away, first recommend a really good wine.' The steward did so, and I ordered a bottle. He looked at us again and asked if we would like to order food as well. 'Of course,' I said. We were lucky, he told us, as there were two portions of wild duck left.

I was dancing with Lilian when I noticed the Military Police approaching our table and stand next to it. We left the dance floor and returned to our place. The man asked for my papers. On examining them, he saluted smartly and left with a smile. As he was leaving, a General of the German Army sitting in a corner beckoned him and said something to him. When our food was served, the steward brought another bottle of the expensive wine that I had ordered. He said it was with the compliments of the General. When I turned to thank him, I saw that he had left. The senior steward gave Lilian a bouquet of flowers with apologies of the management for the inconvenience caused. Overall, it was a wonderful evening.

18 KIMONO*

Netaji and Abid Hasan's Japanese submarine I-29 finally docked at Sabang Port on Weh Island, located to the north of Sumatra, on 6 May 1943. They were put up in a secluded bungalow so that they could rest and recover from their long journey in the cramped and claustrophobic submarine space.

Touching firm ground after such an extended voyage on high sea, they felt as if they had been released from jail after a long confinement. Abid Hasan compared it to his release from Arthur Road prison. His friends had come to receive him in a car. Safrani wanted to walk. But after walking just a short distance he felt as if he had walked a mile and he finally got into the car with a sigh of relief. He recalled that it was a very similar feeling when he came out of the submarine and stepped onto solid ground.

Netaji was getting restless, eager to reach Tokyo as soon as possible. He wanted to expedite the process of negotiating with the Japanese to build his army to liberate India. Netaji and Abid Hasan boarded a Tokyo-bound plane at Sumatra. The plane could not land at Tokyo due to bad weather and got diverted to a military strip near Tokyo. The only place available to stay was a traditional, Japanese style inn, where they were put up for the night.

The Japanese inn was beautiful, clean and tidy. Abid Hasan found a pair of kimonos artfully arranged in a corner—obviously meant for guests after they took a bath and wanted to relax. Abid Hasan took a quick bath. Knowing that Netaji took longer in the bathroom, he decided to take off for a while. He put on a kimono and went out to explore the new area and get a breath of fresh air. As he stepped out of his room, the Japanese maid gave him

---

*Based on Abid Hasan Safrani's unpublished private notes and papers, in custody of Ismat Mehdi.

a rather mischievous smile. The other members of the staff also seemed to be suppressing their laughter while looking at him.

Abid Hasan was a bit puzzled but he went out anyhow and walked leisurely about the neighbourhood that he found to be quite interesting. Everywhere he went he found people laughing when they saw him. Some even tried to talk to him, but he could not understand their language, and neither could they. But he quite liked the way they greeted him by laughing and so he would smile back at them.

When he returned to the inn from his wanderings, his Japanese friends who were waiting for him instantly broke into laughter on seeing him, and said to Netaji, 'Look how your secretary has behaved!'

Abid Hasan could not figure out what the matter was. He had just worn a kimono. When you are in a foreign country, it is nice to wear their traditional clothes. He asked them, what did he do wrong?

They told him that he was wearing the wrong kimono—it was the one meant for ladies!

He had chosen the one that looked beautiful and bright.

19 HAS-SAN*

During their stay in Japan Abid Hasan once ran into big trouble. It almost made Subhas Bose sack him. Let's have it in Hasan's own words.

One afternoon we were sitting in the living room waiting for the office team to arrive. The maid, a beautiful young Japanese girl who looked after our rooms, beckoned me with a sign of her hand and a smile, calling out softly, 'Hasan'. I went to her and she escorted me to my room. There she pointed out to some papers spread out on my bed; I had been busy working that day. I collected them and placed them on the table. She nodded a thank you to me and left.

When I returned, I found Netaji in a furious mood. His face was red with anger.

In a voice almost choking with suppressed rage, he said, 'How often have I told you that you have to be on your guard all the time! Every action of yours reflects on me and my mission. One cannot be careful enough. You will wreck my work and I will not let that happen. I may have to remove you from me immediately.'

I took a little time to decide what I should do. The maid was a nice girl. Disturbed, I meekly asked him what had happened, knowing fully well the cause of his anger.

'What has happened?' asked Netaji. 'Do you mean to tell me that it is natural for that maid to simply call you "Hasan" as if you were her old friend? I abhor this intimacy. I find your conduct unpardonable. I am repeating that I will not tolerate this. I shall send you away.'

Being called 'Hasan' by the young Japanese maid lost all its pleasantness as I wondered what Netaji would think of it. I had

---

*Based on Abid Hasan Safrani's unpublished private notes and papers, in custody of Ismat Mehdi.

been friendly and polite with her but done nothing that might encourage her to be so familiar. I did not find it amusing.

My pride was hurt, and I could not tolerate such harsh words even from Netaji.

'I am sorry, Sir,' I said in a measured tone, 'that I have failed to come up to your expectations. You are of course at liberty to send me away. No explanation is necessary. My sole reason to be with you was to be of assistance to you. If I have failed in that, I have no reason to be here. I belong to the Army and I shall revert there. Shall I leave this instant? All I can say is that I have tried my best to do my duty. I may add that it is not any gesture, action or lapse of discipline on my part that has encouraged this familiarity on the part of the maid.'

'Then I shall report this matter to the officers,' Netaji said.

After a few minutes, the Japanese officers arrived.

Netaji came straight to the point. 'Unfortunately, gentlemen, I have to start this session with a serious complaint.'

The officers were startled. The smiles vanished from their faces and they solemnly enquired what the matter was.

'The maid here on duty is trying to be familiar with my secretary, and this is something I do not appreciate,' said Netaji.

'This certainly is a serious matter,' the senior among them said and added that the issue would be addressed. 'But would you please let us know, Sir, how is she being familiar?'

'Dropping the mister, she has started calling my secretary just Hasan,' said Netaji.

At this, all the Japanese officers broke out into unrestrained laughter. One look at Netaji's face however, and they quickly controlled themselves and explained.

'Sir, the maid is not at fault. In our language and among ourselves we do not refer to you as Mr. Bose but as Bose San. San is equivalent to Mr. but it is added after the name. When we talk of Mr. Hasan, we call him Has-san. Presumably in English he would be called Mr. Has. The maid who addressed him as Has-san means no disrespect. Anyway, we will tell her.'

'No! No!' said Netaji, who was also laughing now. 'Please don't mention this matter to her. I do not want her to lose her composure. I hope Mr. Has here also has no resentment towards her now.'

With that the matter was dropped. However, throughout our stay in Tokyo, these Japanese officers insisted on calling me Mr. Has. And each time they would do so with a mischievous smile.

20 'NETAJI AND THE INDIAN COMMUNAL QUESTION'*

ABID HASAN SAFRANI

A look at the political map today of what was once French West Africa gives us an insight of how it suits an imperial power to proceed with the division of territory when forced to give it freedom. There are in this region of Africa independent and sovereign countries with population varying from about four million people to a little more than half a million. Each country has to bear its burden on defence, internal administration and external relations. With customs barriers erected on their frontiers overnight, each country has to take into serious consideration the capacity of its own internal market before they can venture into creating an industry, however small, and change their status from under-developed to a developing nation.

The widespread sub-continent of India with its vast material and spiritual, especially leadership, potential, together with its Asian consciousness, threatened, once it became free, to become a big power and play its own independent role, which the imperialist power then governing its destiny knew would not be to its liking. This India had to be destroyed. Plans were made to give one of its former provinces its independence. This would have been followed by the independence of other provinces and of course of the native states. Even so, due to the already engendered communal and disruptive feelings there would have been constant bickering among these states without any one of them being able to play any constructive role.

*Originally published in *The Oracle* of January 1979, and reproduced here by courtesy of the Netaji Research Bureau, Kolkata.

Our leaders fully realised this danger and they, especially Mahatmaji, Nehru and Patel, woke up in time to take rigorous action to avoid this balkanisation of the country. Unfortunately, we did not wake up early enough to avoid a major partitioning based on inflated communal dissensions. We had failed to understand the nature and working of communalism.

Communalism is not the disease itself but one of its outward symptoms. Its other symptoms are casteism, groupism, factionalism, regionalism and linguistic fanaticism. The disease itself is the economic malfunctioning in the body politic of our country caused by unequal and disproportionate distribution of the available wealth in the country, leading to large-scale unemployment and massive underemployment. This was acute during the days of the British Raj. Our industry was then limited and its development, especially in new ventures, discouraged. Research in its fields remaining static, our agriculture too followed old patterns and could not expand. These factors in their turn set limits to the development of trade and free professions. There was thus a time when employment, in particular for the educated youth, could be found mainly in government services. With the government being in a position to manipulate it, the basis was thus found for one community to imagine that another was being preferred in obtaining the opportunity of providing for [an individual] himself and his family. It was this grudge, levelled by one group against another, that formed the basic background for communal disharmony.

Netaji was of the opinion that if employment could be found for everyone, then the basic cause of dissentions between the communities would be removed and the way opened for absolute integration. Finding employment for all was not a utopian dream. It could be done by the proper distribution of the available wealth. In the Azad Hind Fauj this wealth was mobilised through increasing donations by all the Indians living in South East Asia. It was then utilised for the distribution of equal rations and uniforms to all ranks. The quantity and quality of the uniforms improved and deteriorated depending on the available funds. The distribution was equal to all—Netaji himself not exempted. When the rations became meagre and at times failed completely, no one grudged because, big and small, all suffered the same fate and given these conditions, my experience is that Indians are capable of tremendous forbearance.

Apart from the rations and uniforms, there was the question of pay. This was not equal for all ranks, but it was as we considered—equitable. The ordinary soldier of the Azad Hind Fauj and the worker of the Azad Hind Dal was paid a salary of Rs 40 a month. I, as a Major received Rs 120 and the generals, including divisional commanders and the Supreme Commander, Rs 250 a month.

From a part of our pay, we augmented our rations. To what extent this was possible one can appreciate considering the fact that a chicken cost at one time Rs 25 and at another Rs 50. Netaji himself set the pattern that no extra money would be channeled in increasing the fare at the table of those who had access to public funds. Half the salaries of those on his personal staff, from himself down to his batman, was given by me personally to the sergeant in the kitchen and proper account of all purchases maintained. This procedure was strictly adhered to and the house being open, the public at large knew that it was indeed being followed.

One may say here that this Spartan way of life could be followed only during a period of emotional upsurge and could not last long. This becomes an academic question and I cannot argue it. I can only say that this period was not at all short, stretching itself over a couple of years. Moreover, Netaji had schemes ready of introducing a planned economy in the country with large-scale nationalisation of industries and enterprises together with rationing of food, cloth and essential commodities all over India. This large-scale mobilisation of national resources held promise of proportionate distribution of wealth and the ultimate employment of everyone in the country.

Simultaneously with these measures, Netaji made it known in repeated statements that allocation of responsibility to individuals, in other words the choice of persons in the large-scale government and government-controlled employment and their promotion in it would depend upon merit and there would be no other criterion for it. This was preached and this was practised, and the results were exhilarating. To further his own cause no individual had to seek group or factional loyalties, nor, having come to power, patronise anyone. Achieving responsibility on merit, we executed it with an efficiency which demanded and received respect from everyone. Groupism and factionalism became with time non-existent in South East Asia.

One regrettable aspect of the rise of nationalism in India was that at an early stage of its development, it became associated with religion as evidenced in the prayer meetings, singing of bhajans etc. In order to find an equally easy approach for the Muslim masses the Khilafat movement was started, which the other nationalists welcomed. This was playing into the hands of the imperialists, who with the passage of time succeeded in facilitating the Muslim League to employ the same sentiments for demanding the separation of the country. Our political future was threatened enough when the British began consulting the Muslim League also, when they were forced to confer with our leaders. It became dark when our leaders also began negotiating with it, giving the Muslim League the required breakthrough and confirming its leaders in their claim of being the spokesmen of the Muslim masses. The demand for separation encouraged other reactionaries in their call for a Hindu Rashtra. All this unleashed the basest feeling in us, which later was to take a deplorable and savage turn.

Netaji divorced religion completely FROM NATIONALISM. Although a deeply religious man himself, he would not permit public display of any religious practice. Religious devotion thus became the individual concern of each person or, if practised in a group, then restricted to the congregational centres set apart for this purpose. There was to be no intermingling of any other sentiments with Netaji's political ideology.

Perhaps an incident from the Königsbrück camp of the German Wing of the Azad Hind Fauj may illustrate this point. Our Legion there had been formed and it was growing. The separate caste kitchens had been abolished and even the smallest units were mixed, not one being composed of men from the same region or religion. We felt really united and one. But one fact disturbed us, namely that those amongst us who prayed had to go their different ways. Some of our men then sat down and composed a common prayer using only the word 'Malik' for God, a term acceptable and dear to all. Composed by devoted men hailing from remote villages this prayer had Kabirian simplicity and charm, appealing to all.

When Netaji came to our camp on one of his periodic visits, we all, Hindus, Muslims, Sikhs and Christians proudly recited in front of him with one voice. We could not even find out his reaction because he seldom betrayed his feelings. We were however convinced that he must have been greatly pleased.

Later, I was called to meet him and taken to task for having encouraged what he called 'this stunt'. 'No' he said, 'I do not want the intermingling of any other sentiment with our national ideology. If you use religion to unite yourself today, you leave the door open for someone to attempt later to separate you using the same sentiment. The men have their congregational centres. Let each go there and pray as much as he wants, but when you all are together you shall cherish and nurture only national sentiments and no other.' Needless to say, the common prayers were scuttled.

In order not to tarnish his purely nationalist ideology, Netaji was determined not to make any compromises, even when our great need for funds was threatened. This policy paid rich dividends as may be gathered from his dealing with the Chettiar priests in Singapore. The Chettiars were a close community as a religious group. This did not hinder them from large-heartedly responding to our appeal for funds and being a rich class, their donations were generously big.

On the first *Dussehra* after his arrival in Singapore, the Chettiar priest asked Netaji to grace the occasion by celebrating the puja at their temple. He, however, brusquely refused the invitation saying he would not step over the threshold of a place which even some Hindus, not to speak of other Indians, were not permitted to cross. This summary dismissal of their priest, we assumed, would alienate all the Chettiars and we would have to forego their contribution. What happened was quite different. The very next day the priest came again to Netaji, this time inviting him to preside over a national political rally to be organised by them in their temple on *Dussehra* day. Netaji naturally accepted it. When on the appointed day we entered the temple, we found it had been thrown open to Indians of all religious denominations and even to the Malays.

'I have always denied' said Netaji on that day 'that there is communalism among the Indian masses, however, much this may be asserted by the imperialists and some self-seeking Indians serving their cause. We are one, belonging to one individual community whatever our individual religion may be and I congratulate the priests of this temple for giving us the opportunity to assert it so demonstratively today.'

It was not enough just to remove the cause of dissention. Our unity had to be affirmed, consolidated and kept alive. This was possible only by achieving emotional integration of our people in a great measure.

To start with it was necessary to have a national anthem. This question when first posed was received with dismay by all of us who had participated in the national struggle. We remembered how time and again our ranks were broken under police lathi charges only to be reformed again with shouts of 'Bande Mataram'. We were second to none in our veneration to the great historic anthem. But we could not sing it and a national anthem that cannot be sung by the common man did not fulfil its purpose. We therefore chose 'Jana Gana Mana' giving it an easy yet martial tune. With this song too we had our difficulty. We could not, with the limited time at our disposal, get our people to learn the Bengali version. Knowing that Tagore would turn in his grave, we rendered the song into Hindustani and poor Hindustani too, I admit. But this version could be taught. Soon it was sung by all.

The flag too had to change. The charkha in it had become the symbol of nonviolence. This had to be dropped. In its stead we introduced the Leaping Tiger, signifying strength, fearlessness and tenacity in the pursuit of our goal. There were no reservations in its acceptance also—except from one elderly man, who was perhaps the spokesman of a group. He claimed to be an old Congressman with a long record as a freedom fighter. 'With the disappearance of the charkha, there goes our seniority also,' he bemoaned. This for the others was yet another welcome virtue of the tiger. Whether one belonged to the old guard or not, the clause of merit would remain operative for the occupancy of any office.

One serious hindrance in seeking emotional integration was the absence of a common greeting. *Namaste*, *Sat Sri Akal*, *Salaam* had all to be dropped, not finding common acceptance apart from the fact that each of these required the submissive bowing of the head accompanied by the equally submissive movement of one or both the hands. We, on the contrary, wanted to stand erect with the head lifted up when greeting even those much senior to us, as soldiers do when greeting their officers. Netaji prodded us on to find such a greeting and we did so. 'Jai Hind' was spontaneously acclaimed, and it became our salutation and war-cry common to every Indian.

One step leads to another; we had to tackle the question of a national language. Though we did not have the time to discard English and start a common official language, attempts were made in this direction. We chose Hindustani in Latin script for the purpose. The emphasis was on Hindustani which meant choosing the simplest words used by the common man, eliminating all abstract Hindi and Urdu overtones. This was to go side by side with English, thus giving Hindi and Urdu-speaking people only a marginal edge over the other. Though Netaji loved Bengalee, he advocated Hindustani in the larger interest. He managed to make others accept it.

One beneficial side effect of the army uniform is that when one meets a man wearing it, it is not possible to pin him down as a member of a particular religion. Noticing this Netaji introduced the khaki trouser and bush shirt as a uniform for the civil organisation also. Later he went further and adopted it as his dress all the time, even when relaxing at home or attending small functions. We all others began to do the same including our women following the example set by Col. Lakshmi Sahgal and her officers of the Rani Jhansi Regiment. The khaki bush shirt and trousers thus became our official, private and social dress common to all without distinction of community, region, personal wealth and social standing of the individuals.

One last step towards our national integration, perhaps the most vital of all, was only started by Netaji but unfortunately could not be pursued with the dedication it deserved due to other matters requiring immediate attention. I refer to the development of the youth movement. The importance of what one learns as a child, especially as regards prejudices and aversions, is known. If the faith of a secular, integrated India is planted in the young it can successfully withstand all storms later. In this belief Netaji started the *Bal Sena*, but we were on the march to Delhi and this organisation was not given the required impetus for survival.

21 'THE TASK AFTER WINNING FREEDOM'*

Netaji Subhas Bose's Speech to a Gathering in Singapore, 1943

We are gathered here in Singapore, all of us, to undertake a task which we all regard as holy: the task of winning freedom for our country. We know the task will be difficult and in fulfilling it we shall have to pay a heavy price. We are prepared to pay that price.

This task of winning the freedom of our country will be a preliminary one. Greater than our duty of winning the freedom of our country will be our bounden duty to keep Mother India independent, sovereign and above all united after we have won our freedom.

I have often said before and I repeat now that we lost our freedom not because we did not put up a fight but only because our struggle was not coordinated. We lost our freedom because the princes and the leaders in India at that time were not united.

This disunity among us has been systematically instigated since then by our enemies. They seek to divide us by inculcating in us the hatred of one province towards another, one religion towards another and one caste and one language towards another. They say we cannot be united; they say the differences in our ranks are fundamental, that they are in our blood and that they cannot be overcome.

---

*On reaching Singapore in 1943, Subhas Chandra Bose addressed a gathering of the Indian diaspora. The text of this speech is reproduced from the unpublished notes and papers of Abid Hasan Safrani, who was present on the occasion.

Even while emphasising all this they too in a strange way accept our unity. When serving the British we are united. We are united in the I.C.S., in the I.P.S. and in the C.I.D. We are united in safeguarding British interests and we are united in getting killed to achieve British imperialism in Iraq and in Egypt and in Europe and here in Malaya and in China. But when it comes to safeguarding Indian interests, they say we are not one people, that we are not all Indians and that we have separate identities.

I have always maintained and declare again that this is not true. I say that this disunity is devoid of all reality and that this is a fiction concocted by our enemies. When we come abroad the people from other parts of the world like the Malays here, the Chinese here and the Japanese here do not call us Bengalis or Malayalis or Hindus or Muslims. We are only Indians to them and in fact too Indians really we are. This disunity among us is a fiction propagated by the British and some of their henchmen who for their own personal gain are prepared to sacrifice the greater interest of the motherland. This so-called disunity is not real. It does not exist.

Look at what has happened today. Till yesterday this place where we are all now sitting side by side was for us as Indians in general a secluded area, entrance to it being open only for the limited members of a certain sect. Till yesterday everybody would believe this separatism was a reality, this discrimination was a reality and that it would never be removed. And today I am here, and you are here, all of us gathered together in this holy precinct by virtue of only being Indians though individually we may be Punjabis or Tamilians, Hindus, Sikhs or Muslims.

I must congratulate the high priest, his colleagues and the trustees of this temple for taking this bold step and making this holy place still holier because it has been thrown open to all of us.

The priests of this temple have fulfilled their duty towards Mother India by inviting us to enter this precinct. Now it is incumbent on us on entering it to remove from our hearts and from our minds such suspicion as may be lurking there about the intentions, motives and feelings of others towards us. Remember it is this suspicion implanted in us by the alien rulers that is the main cause of communal disharmony in India when it erupts from time to time. We must root this suspicion out and have no reserve of any kind in accepting a brother as a brother, a sister as a sister and trusting them implicitly.

What has happened here today will happen in India a hundred times over, a thousand times over, a million times over till we all give proof to ourselves and to the world that we are an indivisible brotherhood gathered together without any discrimination in the lap of Mother India.

I have maintained that without struggle, without sacrifice and without blood our freedom is not worth having. We are happy that we now have our own army, our national army with indivisible rules ready to march fighting into India. When we march one by the side of the other, one getting killed and shedding his blood by the side of the other with Jai Hind as his last words then those of us who remain alive and see India free will guarantee that no dissension shall ever again creep among us. In our struggle we are united, and we shall remain united when we gain our freedom. In our struggle we shall die shouting Jai Hind and we shall celebrate our victory parade at the Red Fort shouting Jai Hind. Jai Hind is not only our slogan, it is also our pledge. Jai Hind is our belief, Jai Hind is our creed. Jai Hind is the expression of our common brotherhood, common belief, common ideology and common aim.

Jai Hind!

22 'THE MEN FROM IMPHAL'*

ABID HASAN SAFRANI

He was all we had, our leader to whom each one of us however humble meant something and who to us all meant everything. He belonged to us, to us all of the Azad Hind Movement and entirely without compromise.

Without any compromise: That was what attached us to him completely. When we came to Malaya and unfurled his banner thousands of Indians hailed him, ready to die at his command. Volunteers he had enough for his army, however large he wanted to make it but there was serious dearth of equipment. For that money was needed. The poor man donated his mite spontaneously and instances were not rare when they gave their all. The men gave the money in their saving bank and the women the jewelry they wore. But our need was great and economics being what they are, we had to depend upon the support of the rich and among the rich known for their generosity towards our cause were the Chettiars.

Then one day the head priest of the Chettiar temple in Singapore, accompanied by other worthies of his order, came to see Netaji and invited him to grace the Dessehra festival to be celebrated in his temple. We were under the impression that his visit was one of courtesy and the invitation therefore came as a surprise. 'What!' he said, 'Come to your temple where even Hindus of other castes are not permitted entry, not to speak of members of other communities who are equally near and dear to

*Originally published in Abid Hasan Safrani, *The Men from Imphal* (Calcutta: Netaji Research Bureau, 1971), 12–22. Reproduced here by courtesy of the Netaji Research Bureau, Kolkata.

me? No Sir, definitely not.' With that the audience was over and the priest was politely led out.

The attitude adopted by Netaji impressed us all deeply. We knew that he was a religious person and we would have taken it only as normal if he had gone for his puja to the temple while those of us in his following should not enter it and would have waited outside for his return. But we still had to learn how absolute and indiscriminating our love had to be for our motherland. In achieving Jai Hind no division among us of any kind was to be tolerated. For this we were prepared to back our leader completely. We would do with less if the Chettiar high priest turned away from us.

But he came back with his colleagues on the eve of Dessehra. He had no appointment but there was something in the look of his eyes which made me bold enough to take him unannounced for the audience he sought. This time he and his friends did not take off their traditional *Chaddar* and tying them round their waists bowed down low with bare upper bodies before Netaji. They stood erect before him and the high priest simply said, 'Sir, tomorrow evening I am holding an Indian national demonstration in my temple. I shall be grateful if you would preside over it.' The invitation was accepted. Nothing further was said or asked.

When we came to the temple I found it filled to capacity with the uniforms of the INA officers and men and the black caps of the south Indian Muslims glaringly evident. At the entrance some priests met us and reverently led the way and we found ourselves before the holy of holies. When Netaji stepped into the sanctuary, I held back but the priest behind me gently but resolutely pushed me in also. I had never performed a puja before but I did what Netaji did, submitting the offerings already prepared for us and being blessed in turn by a tilak on the forehead put there, with a reverent smile on his face, by the high priest himself. As we left the shrine Netaji wiped the tilak from his forehead and so did I.

I do remember the speech Netaji gave on that occasion. The memory I retain is one of an invigorating music as that of a symphony dedicated to the unity of the motherland and the common purpose of all Indians to be united in their effort to establish their identity. And that music echoed in my mind as we marched along on our way to Moulmein. How lucky were we of having this chance of joining with him again. What were we without him? Now we were different. We had a purpose in life. We had something to live for and something to die for. We had acquired a self-respect unknown to many of us before. Perhaps the story of a high-ranking officer in our army can make the meaning more clear than words can convey.

The military knowledge of this officer, his experience, leadership and integrity would have marked him out for an important command that was then being formed, were it not that he, when off duty, was fond of the bottle, and a bottle he was known to find wherever he happened to be, even deep in the jungle. He could not care less what others thought about it. It was therefore no surprise to him when at that time this command had to be given to somebody, he was called to the Supreme Headquarters. He was sure he would be told that he was being superseded. He was surprised however when Netaji started discussing the details of the command with him and then added—'You know now, Colonel, the importance I attach to this command. Well, I have decided to give it to you. I have full confidence in you.' Although taken aback, the Colonel, stubborn and defiant that he was, managed to ask 'Are there any special instructions, Sir?' 'No,' replied Netaji simply, 'none at all. To a man of such sterling qualities like yours I have no special instructions to give.'

The Colonel, with a stern face but eyes dim, stood up at attention and saluted Netaji and said: 'I am grateful to you, Sir, for this trust in me. I assure you, Netaji, that I shall constantly endeavour to justify your trust in me. Incidentally, Sir, for your information I may add that I have stopped drinking.' 'Really?' said Netaji, surprised in his turn, 'Since when have you stopped it, Colonel?' 'From now on, Sir,' the Colonel said and saluting left the room. He does not drink even today.

All that we Indians needed was a call and our conviction that the call was sincere. The response to it was then immediate. I remember a walk I had once not far from Rangoon with Capt. Thevar of the Rani Jhansi Regiment. We went to a hillock and sat there looking at the ground around us. 'Doesn't the countryside remind you of home?' I enquired, adding, 'It looks so typically Indian.' 'I do not know' she replied simply, 'I have never been to India.'

I could not but marvel at all that was happening. Here was a girl in her early twenties, born and educated in Malaya, who had left the care of her parents, the shelter of her home and the prospects of a career, staying a thousand miles away, rifle in hand to fight and prepared to die for a motherland she had not seen. And she was not the only one. There were hundreds of other girls, all from established families and men in their thousands from all walks of life. The allegiance to India of all these overseas Indians, a much maligned body today, when put to excruciating tests, was found to be of a fervour perhaps greater but certainly not less than ours who owed everything to our motherland.

How could we, one and all, fail to respond when he our leader was so absorbed with our cause? He had no identity apart from our community to which he dedicated himself heart and soul. He wore the clothes we wore and he ate the food we ate. Even at his residence, be it in Singapore or Rangoon, when there were no guests, the food served at the table was that issued to every INA soldier both in quality and quantity, supplemented with what we could afford from our meagre salaries. Netaji's contribution being strictly equal to ours. And he worked more than anyone I knew. He hardly retired for the night before two o'clock in the morning and there is no instance to my knowledge when at sunrise he was found in bed.

Perhaps this very absorption with his work helped him in conserving his energies by not letting him expose himself to others, perhaps unnecessary but so human and fatiguing. Thus the three months he spent in the submarine, denied the possibility of personal hygiene, with no room to move even a few steps, shut away from nature, cramped in a space, not only strange and artificial but narrow in the extreme, would have taken a heavy toll of a man enjoying better health than he could claim. But from the day he entered the submarine he started to work and I too could feel on myself what a blessing engrossing work can be. He had so many plans for the struggle in East Asia and they had all to be worked out and, as was his habit, each one in detail.

On the day he was working on a favourite subject, the formation of the Rani Jhansi regiment. He asked me to bring forth all arguments I could, why our women would not respond to his call to go with him to Burma in trousers and bush-shirts rifle in hand. Except at radio stations he never read out his speeches except on solemn and formal occasions, but nevertheless, whenever he could, he drafted them with care and then threw away the composed text, later making such changes as necessary when delivering them. He was on that day busy with his speeches to the Indian women when our submarine sighted an enemy freighter and made preparations to attack it. All the commands were given over the internal communication system and Netaji knew German well enough to follow them clearly. He took an interest in all this but not enough to stop him from his work.

Then something happened which gave me a scare even today. Through the negligence of the man at the controls our submarine surfaced. She came up on the surface just when the order to release the torpedoes was about to be given. Seeing the submarine thus exposed the captain of the freighter, which was now not far removed, reacted immediately and turned his ship in our direction, bore down on us with full speed to ram us. 'Dive!' the Captain shouted his orders, 'Dive! Dive!' But having surfaced by mistake the orders to dive could not be immediately carried out, though ordinarily it would take less than a minute to do so. Moments, as our Captain was reminding in his orders, separated us from sure death and to me it appeared natural that everyone should be scared.

Everyone, I think, was scared and I could imagine what I looked like seeing death reflected in some of the faces I could see. Not everyone was scared, not Netaji. 'Hasan' he remonstrated, 'I have repeated the point twice and you are not noting it down.' 'I am sorry Sir,' I replied much ashamed and went on with violently beating heart and shaking fingers to write down what he calmly dictated.

Meanwhile the freighter roared down on us. There was a jilt and our submarine suddenly turned on one side. For a time we did not know whether we were hit or sinking. After what seemed ages we came to know that we had managed to dive just in time and the freighter could only scratch the railings of our bridge which gave us the jerk.

Later, addressing the crew, the Captain said they all could take a lesson from our 'distinguished guest and his adjutant in facing a sudden crisis involving even death with manly composure'. Even I was included in the praise, who had so shivered with fear. But I was with a great man and my weakness was hidden away in the shadow of his greatness. And the point Netaji was making in the draft of his speech to the women of India, when this incident took place, was that they, given the choice between death and dishonour, had always opted for death. He, however, did not want them to jump into flaming pyres but ride out into the field, sword in hand, as the Rani of Jhansi did. Later in Singapore when he did address our women, I could see a new light glittering in their eyes. The words Netaji spoke were not new. Words to that effect and the response was natural, because the words were being spoken by a man whom they felt they could trust unto death.

Unto death: Yes, this response to his call from his fellow men and women was natural. We knew him and the strength of his resolve. Could he not have rested on his laurels, having being confined to prison and later, when released in due course of time, demand his share of the national tribute? But for him it was derogatory to India's honour to let Britain take advantage of our weakness. He would not accept inaction in jail, however sanctified this has become by prestigious practice. The probability of certain death did not hold him back to get out of jail and out of India, subjecting his already devastated body to extreme physical stress as he, nearly blind without his glasses, wearily dragged himself up and down the Afghan hills.

How many deaths had he not defied to reach us, putting his faith in us, risking even his political honour, more precious to him than life? Yes, he believed in us, the mixed company that we were. Who but he would have put his trust in us, the mercenary soldier who prided himself of faithful service for generations to the foreigner, the professional and businessman who found competition easy and many possibilities to enrich themselves, the plantation tapper who earned his handful of rice by tireless toil, with neither energy or education for any other thought and the student with his grey life and dreams of easy living on his return.

Yet he came. He came and called us to greatness and we found it easy to shirk away our pettiness from us. He swept us with his enthusiasm and his enthusiasm became ours. So what did it matter that we had suffered reverses in Burma. What indeed did it matter to us were we to be annihilated in the last battle we sought under his leadership. The victory he desired and the victory to which he made us all aspire could not elude us.

We had to prove that the picture India then presented to the world was all wrong. And what a dismal and humiliating picture India did present. One group, however small, was opposed to the other but all were united in handing over Mother India in bondage to the foreigner. It was not the handful of foreigners that held us in subjugation. We were handed over in subjugation to the foreigner by Indians themselves—Indians in the civil service, Indians in the police force, and Indians in the army. The honour a conservative and old-fashioned Indian found in becoming a Khan or Rao Saheb was matched by the arrogant pride an educated and emancipated Indian took when a knighthood was conferred on him.

We had to prove to the world, and more so to ourselves, that all this was not true. India was too great a country with many a different people to come out spontaneously with one united action to redeem her honour. India was always great when her leadership was great and her leadership was great when neither its vision was narrowed by regionality or fanaticism nor when its determination was weak or its purpose vague. We had to prove to the world and to ourselves that given correct leadership, we the common people of India would rise as one man to redeem the honour of the motherland. This we did under the leadership of Subhas Chandra Bose.

In these fractured times, when memory is still fresh of the inhuman acts we recently committed, in these frustrating times when India again seems to be a house divided against itself, I believe that there are many who believe it, that it is all not true. We are and shall remain an inseparable whole. This was the message that the roaring tiger of Bengal gave to us not long ago and the people of India, in homage to his uncompromising leadership, accepted the tiger of Bengal as their true emblem of emancipation. The people of India will accept any leadership provided the call remains the same, and the call cannot be but—'Forget not that the grossest crime is to compromise with injustice and wrong.'

Jai Hind.

23 'MODERN ASPECTS OF INDIAN SPIRITUAL CONCEPTIONS'*

ABID HASAN SAFRANI

The early Indian scriptures are said to be Hindu scriptures, the religious scriptures of Hinduism. This statement is true but it does not contain all the truth. There is no word in these scriptures, or in the Sanskrit language for that matter, for either the word *Hindu* or the word *Hinduism*. There is also no word in Sanskrit for *religion* as we understand it. The word used in Sanskrit for religion is *Dharma*, which may best be translated as duty and moral obligation, duty of man toward man and the duty of man towards nature. The early Indian scriptures are thus in their essence a moral code, a code which every Indian may regard as his own early heritage.

We are justified in taking this point of view because Indian spiritual conceptions are the outcome of the efforts neither of one man nor of one generation, nor even of one race. In this context it may be pertinent to enquire what India itself is; but for our present purpose we may limit our efforts to enquire into the nature of Indian thought. Indian thinking has been from the earliest times, and remains today, a fusion and evaluation of many ideas and many concepts both native and foreign. Our mind is not closed to any trend. The evaluation of all the ideas and fusing them with our culture is, however, our own affair.

---

*This is the text of Abid Hasan Safrani's speech that he delivered as Consul General of India, Damascus, at the University of Damascus on Wednesday, 14 December 1960. The manuscript of the speech—which reveals his thinking, beliefs and the kind of person he was—was found with Safrani's unpublished notes, papers and diary (in custody of Ismat Mehdi).

What is known as India today began to take shape at an early period of history. It was born with the birth of our early codified thought, a process spread over a long period after the arrival of the Aryans into India. The fount of Indian spiritual thinking is contained in the *Gita*. The *Gita* has its religious aspects but, at the same time, it is not correct to say that the way of the *Gita* is merely religion. It is much rather the way of duty, a moral code to which everybody has access. It is not religion in so far that it admits of no set beliefs and it bars no one from its folds. Indeed, Shree Krishna says in the *Gita*: 'I accept individuals in particular manner in which they approach me. Whatever may be the path that a man treads, it ultimately leads to and joins my path.' Thus the path of the *Gita* is open to anyone believing whatever he may, provided only that he is sincere in his belief. He may tread any path provided he is sincere in the path he chooses. Every religion in the final analysis is a moral code, where the believers are called to perform their duty in accordance with the higher value accepted by man. Pure religions thus differ from each other only in minor details. But every religion has to face the problem of man trying to shirk his duty and avoiding to work for his salvation by the continuous observance of the prescribed moral code. People would rather be promised salvation by the performance of some ritual or the incantation of some formula. In the profession of every religion there is thus the difference between theory and practice. Tombs of saints, springs of water, any odd place for that matter becomes a pilgrimage where salvation is sought by elaborate rituals through self-appointed priests. Rituals are thus born, and with them dogmas, that dominate the better concept of pure religion and sometimes become religion itself. This process has been noticed in India also. But in India alongside this process there has been a continuous fight against the corruption of religion, a corruption which invariably leads to social injustices.

Social justice, in other words, the safeguard that man should not be exploited by his fellow man to serve the interest of one man or class of self-chosen men, has been a tenet of Indian spiritual belief. We of course have accepted individual merits and the demand for leadership in society at every stage, but we have also accepted that when a self-chosen section of society imposes its will, as birthright, on the rest of mankind then faith itself or Dharma loses its spiritual quality. A corrupt priesthood naturally justifies this debasement of religion and creates a dogma sanctifying the injustice.

In such a contingency the rehabilitation of social justice can be achieved in two ways: either by the abandonment of the temple or by cleansing it of unsocial elements as Jesus did in Jerusalem. In India it has always been the cleansing approach that has been adopted. The temple was not abandoned to the social elements. Gautama the Buddha followed this method six centuries before Christ, and Mohandas Gandhi the Mahatama followed it nineteen centuries after Christ. Both of them were revolutionaries because they found that the society of their time was corrupted by a dogma, the spiritual conceptions of which India acclaims. Both of them, rather than take the downtrodden masses away from the temple, opened the doors of the temple to the masses.

Gandhi's fight would have been incredibly easier if he had started a new religion or created new temples for the millions and millions of Indians, whom a self-interested clerical hierarchy and the vested interests of a feudal landed gentry had condemned as slave labourers and untouchables. But if Gandhi had created new temples, he would have lost his stature both as man and as an Indian. The harmony of India would then have been lost. There would have been a break in the continuity of Indian thinking, of Indian culture and in all that is of value to India. By throwing open to us the temple gates Gandhi has avoided for us the conflict and contradictions that would otherwise have arisen between our spiritual conceptions and the material conceptions that we learn today in modern schools of economics. Gandhi has not only fought the battle of his lifetime but he has paved the way for his successors. Henceforward it will not be the high priests of closed clans that will interpret for our masses our spiritual values, but men like Dr Radhakrishnan who believe in scientific research and in progressive enlightenment.

The fight between free thinking and dogma is a continuous fight for us in India. Our conceptions become blurred from time to time and again we find a redeemer who once again takes us on the straight path. Some of the movements which have plagued mankind, like the inquisition in the past and racialism not long ago, were based on hatred born of ignorance. The base values in man have often had the upper hand in India also, but in India they never had the support of our enlightened intelligentsia and they have always been checked. Some preach hatred and they are heard for a time, but then others preach love and their voices ultimately dominate. We could thus achieve our independence without carrying over in our young republic any hatred for a former adversary—and we can maintain our independence without nurturing hatred towards any country or any movement.

Modern times are putting greater demands on us, on Indian society and on the Indian community. The pace of industrialisation is increasing, with the state appearing as the greatest enterpriser of all. This will put great stress on us, but we can be confident. We are not only building atomic reactors and giant steel plants but we are simultaneously reforming and revitalising the villages of India in a programme which has equal priority in our national planning. And while India is getting accustomed to the new sounds of our young industry, one man is walking alone from one village to another covering the length and breadth of India, clad in loin cloth and preaching the doctrine of love. When this man, Vinoba Bhave, passes near a big city, State Ministers go to meet him and our Prime Minister and our President—and they go to meet not a divine or a saint but a man who believes that an Indian interpretation can be given to values different from those taught in the school of economics, an interpretation other than those contained in the pamphlets of political parties.

It may appear a vainglorious boast to say that our spiritual conceptions can meet the challenge of modern times, but our past and recent history entitles us to this belief. In the past the major part of India was knit into a close empire by an emperor, Ashoka, who fought but one battle only to renounce war for ever. And he succeeded in uniting the people of India by love. It is no wonder that we have chosen as the emblem of our republic the emblem of Ashoka, the wheel of duty, the dynamism of movement, a promise that India would no more resist change and that she must move and go forward.

About the time of Ashoka, Indian culture and Indian influence spread abroad, mainly to South East Asia. Sanskrit words form a very high percentage of the Thai language even today and temples in Thailand, Cambodia and Indonesia show striking examples of Indian influence. Indians migrated to these parts in thousands and it is said that Indian States existed at one time in these parts. But there is no record of any general or admiral that conquered these territories, nor that any of these states paid tribute to India or were in any other manner regarded as colonies of India. Our relations with these countries were based on the principles of non-interference in internal matters, non-aggression and respect for their sovereignty—principles which have now been enlarged into the Five Principles which guide our foreign relations with all countries today. When we talk of non-alignment with any power bloc today and of equal friendship with all then for us it is not a matter of expediency but a cardinal belief.

Similarly in our internal affairs also we are not tormented by the new theories, already turned into dogma, governing society and social relationship. We do not feel the necessity of building new temples—our old temples have been thrown open to us. There is with us no conflict between our belief and our practice. The equality of man, the equality of the human being rather, has been established in India as our unalienable right. We could thus for instance with the greatest ease accept the modern position of women in our society.

The emancipation of women in India had its roots not in any new social doctrine but in our age-old traditions, in our spiritual beliefs. In the mythology of other nations women are allotted roles of goddesses of love and beauty and other feminine and mystic conceptions. In the Indian pantheon, however, women were allotted roles which could be the envy of any modern aspirant to a Cabinet post. We do not have a god of war, but a goddess. Similarly goddesses, and not gods, were the chief deities of Education and of Wealth—or, in our modern terminology, of Finance. But then India fell into a slumber and with the loss of our dignity the woman in India lost her freedom. A widow was not allowed to remarry. A tortured wife was refused the right to divorce and the daughter the right to her inheritance. But when India awakened it was but natural that our mothers, sisters and daughters should reawaken with us. I do not know of any struggle for the emancipation of our women. We, both men and women, struggled together for India's emancipation and when our society was emancipated, we, men and women, were emancipated together. It is not because of any new social doctrine but because of our own ancient tradition that a widow today remarries, a tortured wife takes her divorce and our daughters inherit our properties as our sons do. It is no wonder therefore that our sisters compete with us today in public service appointments. It is no wonder that we have today a woman Deputy Minister of Finance, a woman Deputy Minister of Interior, a woman as Deputy Minister of External Affairs, a woman as Chief Justice of a State, a woman, who was at one time the President of United Nations General Assembly, as our High Commissioner in London, and a woman as a Governor of a major state.

All this is happening in India and it is happening not because of any new doctrines but because of our own spiritual conceptions. Sometimes our conceptions get distorted but each distortion finds a redeemer. There was for instance at one time an attempt to differentiate the Hindu Indian from the Muslim Indian. The attempt appeared at one time to succeed. But at this crucial time when Indian spiritualism was put to test we had a redeemer and our redeemer was a firm believer in Indian spiritual conceptions. Rather than live and see one Indian being discriminated against another he preferred to sacrifice his own life. Gandhi's body was consecrated to the fire and his ashes were strewed, as were the ashes of the Buddha strewn 2,500 years ago, in all the rivers and streams of India. His ashes were not strewn in vain. On the 26th of January 1950, representatives from the banks of all these rivers and streams of India assembled in Delhi proclaiming India a Sovereign Democratic Republic and securing to all citizens:

JUSTICE, social, economic and political;
LIBERTY of thought, expression, belief, faith and worship;

> EQUALITY of status and of opportunity;
> and to promote among them all FRATERNITY assuring the dignity of the individual and the unity and integrity of the Nation.[1]

These conceptions are not new in India and their acceptance involves no search of heart on our part. They have the sanction of our scriptures and we have now learned and enlightened men, and not priests believing in dogma, to ensure that the scriptures will continue to be correctly interpreted. Every Indian can rest assured of his right to equality, his right to freedom, his right against exploitation, his right of freedom of religion, his cultural and educational rights, his rights to property and his right to constitutional remedies. We can therefore face our future with equanimity, we can look forward to all the industrialisation in India without fear of any loss to our spiritual conceptions.

Jai Hind!

NOTE

1 'Preamble', *Constitution of India, 1950*. Available at https://www.constitutionofindia.net/constitution_of_india/preamble (accessed 25 September 2022).

24 'ON A SLOW BOAT WITH SAFRANI'*

GEETA DOCTOR

To the rest of the world, he might have been a freedom fighter and a soldier who fought alongside Netaji, but to us he was always 'Uncle Safrani'.

Only much later did we realise that his real name was Zain-al-Abdin, or Abid Hasan as he preferred to call himself, and that the stories he told us of his days in the Indian National Army were actually true.

'Compared to us, Safrani was a man of the world,' says my Mother, looking back on the first time that my parents met him, in 1948, on board a ship that was taking them to start the first of the embassies that were just being opened.

Safrani was bound for Cairo, my parents were due to get off at Genoa and make the rest of the trip by land to Paris.

What they did not know then was that they had been booked on a cargo ship. Some cabins had been hastily converted to accommodate First-Class passengers. The ship would take the long route, going up the Persian Gulf, stopping at various ports to unload goods.

For my young parents who were leaving the country for the first time, with two small girls—my sister Surya who was two years old, and I who was five—on a ship belonging to the Scindia Steamship Company as it was known then, Safrani was a wonderful guide. They had never been beyond Indian shores.

Safrani on the other hand was not only a member of the old Hyderabad elite, but had also studied for a while in Germany and

*Originally published in *The Hindu*, 23 March 2002. Reproduced with minor edits with the kind permission of Geeta Doctor.

travelled all over South-East Asia as Secretary to Subhas Chandra Bose.

'Safrani was one of those men who could make friends with all kinds of people. He was all over the ship. When it docked, he would be the first to get off and go straight to the bazaars, and return by evening with all manner of beautiful things. He was also a scholar who spent long hours with his Persian and Urdu poetry. There was nothing he did not know and seeing how raw we were, he made it his business to educate us in all the finer points of life. For instance, when we docked at the port of Basra he ran ashore and bought so many carpets that he ran out of money. But this did not worry him, he just made arrangements to borrow money on credit so that he could buy more,' recalls my Mother.

In the evenings when the ship was at sea, he would take us to the topmost deck and point out the stars and whisper stories to us about all the ancient sailors like Sindbad who had crossed these very seas. To us, he would become like Sindbad the Sailor himself. During the day, dolphins would follow us racing by our side, while as we made our way into Aden, where the local Indians received us like fabulous guests who had been sent by the newly independent Government of India to conquer the world, Safrani showed us how to be gracious in accepting the hospitality of strangers, who could also be family.

At Port Said, he transformed himself into an Arab prince, bargaining with the chattering hordes of intrepid vendors who climbed up from their small boats into the ship, teaching my parents to sip bitter coffee from small glasses and to taste the sticky sweet lumps of baklava.

By the time the ship sailed into the Mediterranean, Safrani had become the perfect European gentleman, as debonair as David Niven, as effusive as Signor Peperino, with his flowing moustache and his ability to charm the ladies with his manner of bowing down to kiss a hand.

It was also, he said, a way in which he kept track of some of his possessions, the beautiful carpets, the pieces of porcelain and small paintings that he had left with us as a token of his friendship. 'I want you to enjoy them as long as you like and when I need to sell something, I will come and collect a carpet or two.'

We were the guardians of his generosity. For though he bought beautiful things with the lavish abandon of an oriental Pasha, his house was always so full of people that he had quite often to sell them to keep the coffers flowing.

He left one ceramic vase with us. It still stands on a pedestal in a corner, converted now into a lamp stand, its deep blue and copper red tones changing colour with the reflection of the light. 'It's a very rare vase from China. Don't ever sell it,' he advised, though Safrani himself regularly sold many of his most cherished possessions.

When we lived in Geneva, he happened to be in Bern. His boss at that time was a dog-lover of epic proportions, so every evening as we stood beside him and listened, he talked to the dog, a large Alsatian, who had been left behind in his care, in Urdu, on the telephone. On another occasion, he told us how the dog had finally died and he was 'Chief Mourner' who conducted the funeral honours. 'It was a very touching occasion. I was so moved, I jumped into the open grave and recited some prayers over the dog's body that I held in my own arms, before laying him into the earth,' he told us. Since he was laughing so much at the memory, we never knew whether any of this was true. Or whether like all the stories he had told us in the past, they were the stuff of the legendary quality that he wove around himself.

'He never mentioned his life with the INA, let alone the story that he had been the one to propose the greeting, "Jai Hind!"' remarks my Mother, 'Though it sounds very typical of him. He was a free spirit.'

Much later, when one of us was passing through Denmark, where he was the Ambassador, we enjoyed the full force of Safrani's hospitality. He drove to the airport himself and though when we reached his house, it seemed to be so full of guests that evening that he had to find a room for us right up in the attic, it was as always a fabulous evening. The dinner when it arrived was as full and rich as one of the tables from the days of the old Hyderabad style hospitality. He always managed to have as a hostess one of his beautiful nieces from Hyderabad, who would quietly attend to the guests and see that no one was without food and drink.

When it was over, he insisted that we should go and enjoy the 'Tivoli Gardens' that was the star attraction of Copenhagen. As we looked at the giant Ferris wheels and the nightly display of fireworks exploding over the skyline of the city, Uncle Safrani had become like Barnum, a grand ring-master presiding over the 'Greatest Show on Earth'.

And then we did not see him again.

We had heard that he had returned to his family home after retirement and become a gentleman farmer.

This is my final memory of him.

On a visit to a silk weaving unit on the outskirts of Hyderabad I found that someone had started a small farm, and on it a school for the children of the nearby village.

The owner, who had died sometime back, had created an enchanted garden of fruit trees. The fields next door were covered with jasmine bushes, dotted with fat creamy jasmine buds that the children from the school came to harvest in the early morning. The air was filled with their fragrance as all over the field the butterflies were busy doing their own kind of harvesting.

One of Safrani's nieces, a really beautiful woman even in her later age, was running a weaving centre. She was preoccupied in reviving some of the old Hyderabadi silk and cotton weaving traditions, and did not have much time to talk. On her table was a photograph of a familiar face, the same moustache, the full lips ready to form themselves into a kiss, the all-embracing smile, the jaunty glint in the eye.

'Safrani!' I exclaimed.

The beautiful niece, still glowing in her old age, looked at the picture. 'My Uncle,' she said quietly.

25 'REPORTING THE REVOLT IN IRAQ'*

PREM BHATIA[1]

On 14 July 1958, a secret military group led by Brigadier Abd al-Karim Qasim overthrew the monarchy of Iraq. The Indian Embassy in Baghdad was without an ambassador at that moment. Abid Hasan Safrani in his capacity of Chargé d'Affaires was responsible. There were angry questions in Parliament about the Embassy being without an ambassador at such a crucial juncture. Members of Parliament felt that Indian interests could not be served with junior diplomats.

Pandit Jawaharlal Nehru, who also held the portfolio of External Affairs, responded.

> Both Abid Hasan Safrani, the Charge d'Affaires in Baghdad and Mr Godfrey Jensen, the Information Officer in Beirut, whose advance knowledge of the recent events in Iraq and Lebanon conformed to the highest standards of diplomatic reporting have another common distinction. Both have suffered in the past from an inadequate appreciation of their merits through assessment under a standardised bureaucratic system. Both are rather unconventional persons, but they are full of initiative and courage and capable of making friends without necessarily wearing a permanent diplomatic mask of insane politeness. In making a personal mention of their qualities, my intention is not to secure publicity for their good work, but to emphasise that the younger elements among our representatives abroad include some excellent people who deserve support and encouragement.

---

*Prem Bhatia, 'The Political Scene—Tragedy and Lessons of the Revolt in Iraq', *The Statesman*, 22 July 1958. Excerpt reproduced here by courtesy of *The Statesman*.

Thanks to Mr Safrani's knowledgeable reporting, the Government was among the best-informed Governments of the world about the shape of things to come in Iraq. By comparison I was reminded of the very painstaking briefing given to me in Baghdad three months ago by the head of a leading Western mission who refused to believe, despite the evidence that was even then available, that Iraq was sitting on a volcano. I remember asking this gentleman what he thought was the general public reaction in that country to President Nasser. Without the slightest trace of hesitation, the diplomat concerned told me that the UAR President was universally hated except of course by "a few irresponsible younger people".

When I brought to the notice that fact that only a few days earlier a long queue at a small shop in a provincial town had waited patiently to buy President Nasser's portrait—with the full knowledge that they might have to go to prison—the Western diplomat exclaimed: "Nonsense! Only the other day I was present at a party when Nasser's name was mentioned. The Iraqis around me spat on Persian rugs". One only hopes that this blindness to the facts of life was not reflected in the reports this diplomat was sending to his own country.

NOTE

1. Prem Narain Bhatia (1922–1995) was an Indian diplomat, and a reputed journalist who served as the editor of several newspapers, including *The Statesman*, *The Times of India*, and *The Indian Express*. He was India's High Commissioner to Kenya (1965–69), and to Singapore (1969–73).

26 ...ALL THANKS TO ZAINU MANNA*

SAJID MAHMOOD

I got married to Abid Hasan Safrani's grandniece in December 1989. Over five and a half years had passed since his demise, but his towering personality and presence could still be felt, influencing the lives of his family. That is how I came to know him. I came to know him through my wife Sara, through my mother-in-law Dr Ismat Mehdi, through my wife's aunt Suraiya Khala and many other family relatives and friends.

Recently, when senior members of his family decided to put together this book about him, I was assigned the task of editing it. While reading to edit I would often get lost in thoughts about him. At the end of it I feel I know him better.

The family lovingly called him Zainu Manna or simply Manna. 'Zainu' must have come from his name Zain-ul-Abdin, but I have no idea about 'Manna'. It just sounded good, especially the affection and warmth with which people talk about him.

My wife Sara would often talk about what he meant to her. During her student days, every weekend she would change multiple buses to reach his farm. He would teach her varied things like, how to make different kinds of soups, how to care for roses, how to graciously thank those who gave her a gift. Sara's thank you notes and letters of condolences were always very touching—all thanks to Manna.

He narrated to her his experiences at the Sabarmati Ashram, explaining that Gandhiji's strength did not come solely from the concept of non-violence but more from the concept of gaining freedom from fear.

---

*Reflections of a person who never met or saw Abid Hasan Safrani.

He told her how Netaji believed in the danger of mixing personal faith with national objectives. He talked about Netaji's tenacity and passion towards achieving objectives that one staunchly believed in—for him it was the freedom of his beloved country.

Most of all, Manna taught her the strength of humility. I carry many of his thoughts that were passed on to me through Sara. During his diplomatic assignments, Manna would ask either his mother, his sister or a niece to stay with him to perform the role of a hostess for official functions. Dr Ismat Mehdi, my mother-in-law, took her turn to be with him in Bern and in Baghdad. Manna fine-tuned her abilities in hosting. Even today, her teas and dinners are perfectly choreographed.

Much to her irritation as a young girl who wanted to enjoy the cities, he pushed her into courses in French, German and Arabic. Perhaps he secretly hoped that she would make a career with the *corps diplomatique*. But all that irritation was finally worth it. Manima (Dr Mehdi) excelled in her assignments at the Arabic Services of All India Radio and later as the head of the Arabic Department at the Central Institute of English and Foreign Languages (CIEFL, now English and Foreign Languages University or EFLU), Hyderabad. During her tenure at CIEFL she was sent as Director of the Maulana Azad Centre for Indian Culture in Cairo. In 2004, the President's Award for Arabic was conferred on her—all thanks to Manna.

My wife and I often visited 'Manna's Farm' to meet up with Suraiya Khala and Chhoti, Suraiya Khala's aunt. It was an extraordinary experience to walk through the 'factory' and see all those weavers working on their looms. There would be piles of beautiful handloom products lying about that one would not usually find in any shop: from rich durries and fabrics of ikat to finely woven gadwal and uppada jamdani saris to exquisitely patterned himroo and mashru fabrics.

Distraught when her marriage did not work out, Suraiya Khala returned to Hyderabad. Manna immediately came to her aid—he renovated a shed to house weavers so that she could utilise her expertise in handlooms. She had worked under doyens of handloom and handicraft like Pupul Jayakar, Martand Singh, Lakshmi Jain and Kamaladevi Chattopadhyay. Her knowledge, passion and talent were now being put to excellent use.

Suraiya Khala was doing what she loved best. I would enviously recall George Bernard Shaw's quote: 'lucky are people who can make a living off their hobby'. Besides, so many rare and vanishing weaves were given a new lease of life and developed further—all thanks to Manna.

There was another person in the family who became a favourite friend of mine: Sumanta Banerjee, a journalist married to my wife's aunt. He had a very close association with Manna. They would exchange letters quite often. Sumanta treasures these letters more than a traditional woman would treasure family jewels. I had an opportunity to read a few of them. Some are hilarious, some serious, while others reflect a very clear thinking on different issues. They all reflect Manna's multi-faceted personality.

This reminds me of a letter I once read that Manna wrote to a niece of his. It was a very personal letter but it had a section on the ever-raging controversy about Netaji's death. Manna sounded a bit irritated with all the stories going around about Netaji being alive and in hiding. Manna had worked very closely with Netaji, including spending months with him in a submarine. Netaji had travelled through the hostile North West Frontier, Afghanistan and Soviet Russia in order to reach Germany, with a British assassination team biting at his heels. He had broached controversial issues with a man no less than Hitler, and impressed upon the Japanese Prime Minister Hideki Tojo that the INA would fight for their own objectives, and not Japan's. Netaji had fearlessly traversed dangerous grounds in single-minded pursuit of his goal, with the full knowledge that he might be killed at any moment. He was completely unafraid of dying.

Why would such a person hide if he was alive and if he had returned to India?

These stories seem to be more to do with the phenomenon of seeking fifteen minutes of fame.

To conclude, while going through the draft of the book, some questions arose in my mind. Did the British leave in a hurry because of the Quit India movement? Or because of the impact of the INA's activities on the armed forces of British India? Or did they leave because they had been devastated by the World War? I think it was the combined effect of all three factors, among others. The new government of independent India did the right thing then in declaring all the INA soldiers as freedom fighters.

Today it is important that the post-Independence generations of India too must know about these exemplary and brave heroes in equal measure. This book is an attempt at doing that.

Jai Hind!

27 QAUMI GEET: SHUBH SUKH CHAIN

'Vande Mataram' was often sung at protest meetings, but it was difficult to memorise and its language was not understood by most people. Lakshmi Sahgal favoured 'Jana Gana Mana' based on Tagore's poem 'Bharoto Bhagyo Bidhata'. Netaji also liked it but it had the same problem; it was written in Sanskritised Bengali.

Therefore Netaji asked Abid Hasan Safrani and Mumtaz Hussain, a writer with Azad Hind Radio, to derive a Hindustani version of 'Jana Gana Mana'. Captain Ram Singh Thakuri was asked to compose the music to a martial tune with a rousing, inspiring tone. The result was 'Shubh Sukh Chain', that was adopted as the *Qaumi Geet* of the Indian National Army.

Shubh sukh chain ki barkha barse, Bharat bhaag hai jaaga
Punjab, Sindh, Gujarat, Maratha, Dravid, Utkal, Banga
Chanchal sagar, Vindhya, Himalaya, neela Jamuna, Ganga
Tere nit gun gayen, tujhse jivan payen, har tan paaye asha
Suraj ban kar jag par chamke Bharat naam subhaga
Jai Ho! Jai Ho! Jai Ho! Jai, Jai, Jai, Jai Ho!

Sab ke dil mein preet basaaey teri meethi baani
Har sube ke rahne waale, har mazhab ke praani
Sab bhed aur farak mita ke, sab gode mein teri aake
Goonthe prem ki mala
Suraj ban kar jag par chamke Bharat naam subhaga
Jai Ho! Jai Ho! Jai Ho! Jai, Jai, Jai, Jai Ho!

Subh savere pankh pakheru tere hi gun gayen
Baas bhari bharpur hawaein jeevan mein rut layen
Sab mil kar Hind pukare, Jai Azad Hind ke nare
Pyaara desh hamara
Suraj ban kar jag par chamke Bharat naam subhaga
Jai Ho! Jai Ho! Jai Ho! Jai, Jai, Jai, Jai Ho!

To blessed showers of joy and peace, behold India has risen
Punjab, Sindh, Gujarat, Maratha, Dravid Utkal Banga,

The vast restless ocean, the Yamuna-Ganga blue,
The Vindhya and Himalaya sing your eternal virtues
From you they get life
From you every heart gets hope
May the glorious name of India shine upon the world like the sun
Glory! Glory! Glory! May glory ever be yours!

Your sweet tongue kindles love in every heart
Followers of every faith, inhabitants of every part
Shedding all differences and divisions gather in your lap
Like your children, weaving garlands of amity and love
May the glorious name of India shine upon the world like the sun
Glory! Glory! Glory! May glory ever be yours!

Each sacred dawn the birds sing your praise
The fragrant winds breathe life to every season
All hail Hind! This great and beloved land of ours
Let calls of 'Jai Azad Hind!' rend the skies
May the glorious name of India shine upon the world like the sun
Glory! Glory! Glory! May glory ever be yours!

However, on 24 January 1950, a part of 'Jana Gana Mana' in its original form was adopted as the National Anthem of the Republic of India.

28 EPILOGUE

The narration of Abid Hasan Safrani's life shows how well synced he was with Netaji's thinking and his beliefs. His ideals of nationalism, love and sacrifice for one's country and his belief in the value of freedom were very much in line with Netaji's own. It would not be wrong to say that while he was deeply influenced by Netaji, in many instances Safrani too influenced Netaji.

Lamentably, at an early stage of its development, nationalism and the freedom struggle in India became closely associated with religion, as manifested in prayer meetings, singing of bhajans, religious congregations and the like. It gave rise to the Khilafat movement, which was at the time welcomed by other nationalists. With the passage of time, however, it also created the grounds for the Muslim League to employ the selfsame sentiments for demanding the separation of the country on religious grounds. Their demand encouraged other reactionaries in their call for a Hindu Rashtra.

Today one can perhaps understand better in retrospect why Subhas Bose, who was deeply religious himself, advocated so fiercely and passionately against mixing religion and personal faith with patriotism and nationalism—he was indeed farsighted.

The Partition of the country into India and Pakistan resulted in millions of deaths, causing untold bloodshed, displacement and trauma, leaving deep scars on both sides that have not healed fully even after seventy-five years. Abid Hasan Safrani, disheartened and disillusioned by the Partition and with the collapse of Netaji's efforts and by his untimely death, lived to see only a few ideas that they had together worked for and fought hard to be accepted in the emergent new India. In the post-Independence period, he continued his efforts by joining the Indian diplomatic service to work on foreign relations based on mutual respect, autonomy, peace and friendship.

Had the thinking of Netaji and Abid Hasan prevailed, India would have been on a different trajectory and platform today. Their humane and holistic vision of the nation and its people remains as a guiding light to what could be a far better future, if only we have the eyes to see it and the wisdom and the courage to embrace it.